P9-CLU-939

Generation on a Tightrope

The Jossey-Bass
Higher and Adult Education Series

Generation on a Tightrope

A Portrait of Today's College Student

Arthur Levine
Diane R. Dean

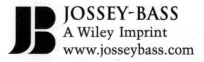
JOSSEY-BASS
A Wiley Imprint
www.josseybass.com

Copyright © 2012 by John Wiley & Sons, Inc. All rights reserved.

Published by Jossey-Bass

A Wiley Imprint

One Montgomery Street, Suite 1200, San Francisco, CA 94104-4594—www.josseybass.com

No part of this publication may be reproduced, stored in a retrieval system, or transmitted in any form or by any means, electronic, mechanical, photocopying, recording, scanning, or otherwise, except as permitted under Section 107 or 108 of the 1976 United States Copyright Act, without either the prior written permission of the publisher, or authorization through payment of the appropriate per-copy fee to the Copyright Clearance Center, Inc., 222 Rosewood Drive, Danvers, MA 01923, 978-750-8400, fax 978-646-8600, or on the Web at www.copyright.com. Requests to the publisher for permission should be addressed to the Permissions Department, John Wiley & Sons, Inc., 111 River Street, Hoboken, NJ 07030, 201-748-6011, fax 201-748-6008, or online at www.wiley.com/go/permissions.

Limit of Liability/Disclaimer of Warranty: While the publisher and author have used their best efforts in preparing this book, they make no representations or warranties with respect to the accuracy or completeness of the contents of this book and specifically disclaim any implied warranties of merchantability or fitness for a particular purpose. No warranty may be created or extended by sales representatives or written sales materials. The advice and strategies contained herein may not be suitable for your situation. You should consult with a professional where appropriate. Neither the publisher nor author shall be liable for any loss of profit or any other commercial damages, including but not limited to special, incidental, consequential, or other damages. Readers should be aware that Internet Web sites offered as citations and/or sources for further information may have changed or disappeared between the time this was written and when it is read.

Jossey-Bass books and products are available through most bookstores. To contact Jossey-Bass directly call our Customer Care Department within the U.S. at 800-956-7739, outside the U.S. at 317-572-3986, or fax 317-572-4002.

Wiley also publishes its books in a variety of electronic formats and by print-on-demand. Some material included with standard print versions of this book may not be included in e-books or in print-on-demand. If the version of this book that you purchased references media such as CD or DVD that was not included in your purchase, you may download this material at http://booksupport.wiley.com. For more information about Wiley products, visit www.wiley.com.

Library of Congress Cataloging-in-Publication Data

Levine, Arthur, author.
    Generation on a tightrope : a portrait of today's college student / Arthur Levine and Diane R. Dean.—First edition.
        pages   cm.—(The Jossey-Bass higher and adult education series)
    Includes bibliographical references and index.
    ISBN 978-0-470-37629-4 (hardback); ISBN 978-1-118-22015-3 (ebk.);
    ISBN 978-1-118-23383-2 (ebk.); ISBN 978-1-118-25862-0 (ebk.)
        1. College students—United States.   2. College students—United States—Attitudes.
3. College students—Political activity—United States.   4. Education, Higher—Social aspects—United States.   I. Dean, Diane R., 1967- author.   II. Levine, Arthur. When hope and fear collide. continues (work):   III. Title.
    LA229.L417   2012
    378.1'98—dc23

                                                                                2012016933

Printed in the United States of America

THIRD EDITION

HB Printing   10 9 8 7 6 5 4 3 2

CONTENTS

We dedicate this book to our spouses, Linda Fentiman and John Giglio, both educators, and to our children, Jamie Levine, who is teaching today's college students; Rachel Levine, who graduated from college in 2010 and is one of the people we are writing about; and Andy and Katy Giglio, who are the college students of the future. We love you very much.

PREFACE

It's a straight line. Which rolls on itself.
Which sways. Which sags.
Which vibrates . . . Ready to explode.
To dissolve. To dissolve me.
To choke me. To swallow me.
To throw me silently across the void . . .

—DESCRIPTION OF TIGHTROPE WALKING BY THE
MAN WHO WALKED BETWEEN THE WORLD
TRADE CENTER TOWERS, PETIT (2008)

THIS IS A portrait of a generation on a tightrope. Today's college students are struggling to maintain their balance as they attempt to cross the gulf between their dreams and the diminished realities of the world in which they live. They are seeking security but live in an age of profound and unceasing change. They desperately want the economic opportunity their parents enjoyed but are coming of age during a deep recession with reduced career prospects. They want to believe in the America Dream and are optimistic about their personal futures but they are pessimistic about the future *of* the country. They want to be autonomous grown-ups but seem more dependent on their parents and the adults around them than any modern generation. They want intimacy—a partner and a family—but they are isolated, weak in face-to-face communication skills and live in a hook-up culture. They want to play by the rules but they don't know the rules and the rules are in flux because of the dramatic changes in our economy, the rise of new technologies, the condition of our public and private institutions, and a world growing flatter. They want to live in an Internet world, a digitally connected globe but the adults and social institutions around them are analog or digital immigrants, including their blackboard universities.

This is a generation that thinks of itself as global citizens but knows little about the world and acts locally. It is the most diverse generation in collegiate history with the strongest relationships between races but they have limited interest in talking about race or reaching across political or generational divides.

This is a story about how we help today's undergraduates cross the abyss that threatens to dissolve and swallow them, and how we can work with them to ensure that they will help us all to create the diverse, global, digital information economy of the twenty-first century.

This book seeks to portray a generation of college students who were born, grew up, and will live their lives in a nation undergoing a transformation from an analog, national, industrial society to a global, digital, information economy. The portrait is a composite, a picture of a generation, not of the individuals who make up that generation. The portrait is multifaceted, a report on a generation's attitudes, values, and experiences replete with the contradictions and inconsistencies that are part of the lives of all human beings. The portrait is complex, looking backward and forward across a span of more than two centuries with multiple historic anchor points and a number of different comparison groups.

This preface is intended to provide an overview of what we learned about today's college students in the course of our research and to touch briefly on the implications of what we found for parents, schools, colleges, government, employers, and the host of institutions that touch the lives of young people.

What we discovered about this generation is that, though it is significantly different from its predecessors, it shares much in common with them. Today's undergraduates and the students who attended college before them were optimistic about their personal futures, pessimistic about the nation's future, committed to the American Dream, little involved in campus life, disenchanted with politics and government, more issue oriented than ideological, engaged in community service, utilitarian in their goals for college, weak in academic skills, beneficiaries of inflated grades, heavy users of psychological counseling services, consumer-oriented regarding higher education, and partial to sex and alcohol, among other things.

This finding challenges the American tendency to view every generation of college students as unique and to focus on the characteristics that distinguish them from their peers of the past. It also points to work that remains incomplete. Many of the challenges facing current college students were challenges for their predecessors but we have not come to grips with them. Parents have not been able to teach their children to be more responsible about their health. Schools have not improved their students' academic skills. Colleges have continued to inflate undergraduate grades. Our political leaders have not given college students any more reason to trust government or be hopeful about the future of the country. It's a finding that reaffirms the critical roles of parents, schools, colleges, government, and all of the other institutions in the lives of young people. They are responsible for raising, educating, developing, enabling, and supporting our children to live satisfying and contributing lives to the fullest extent of their capacity as individuals, family members, neighbors, workers, citizens, followers, and leaders.

We also discovered many things that are significantly different about today's college students. They are described in the following sections.

Today's Undergraduates Are the First Generation of Digital Natives

The students of the 1990s were a transitional generation strad-dling old and new worlds—analog and digital, national and global, industrial and information economies. In contrast, cur-rent students have their feet firmly planted in the new world. This poses an extraordinary challenge to most colleges and universi-ties, which remain largely in the old world, educating an Internet generation in a culture of blackboards. Higher education lags far behind its students technologically and pedagogically and must transform itself if it is to educate current undergraduates for the world in which they will live.

Today's College Students Are the Most Diverse Generation in Higher Education History

Current undergraduates are more diverse demographically than their predecessors; they grew up in a nation in which many of the historic glass ceilings that existed for women, people of color, and gays have cracked; they believe the country has made real progress in race, ethnic, and gender issues; and they are more comfortable than past students with multiculturalism and diversity. Undergraduates are global in orientation but have little knowledge about the world. These findings present colleges and universities with an opportunity to translate their rhetoric about multiculturalism and diversity into reality and the need to internationalize their programs.

Contemporary Undergraduates Are at Once More Connected and More Isolated Than Their Predecessors

Today's college students have extraordinarily close ties with their parents and are in 24/7 contact with a tribe of friends, family, and acquaintances via social media, yet they are more alone in many of the activities they pursue. The image that comes to mind is a group of students walking across campus together, each on their cell phone chatting with other people. Today's undergraduates are weak in interpersonal skills, face-to-face communication skills, and problem-solving skills. This finding raises red flags for parents, schools, colleges, and employers with regard to child-rearing, education, and personnel policies.

Current Students Are Facing the Worst Economy in Recent Memory with Unrealistic Aspirations for the Future

Today's undergraduates believe the economy is the most important issue facing the country. More are working and more are working longer hours. They are taking fewer credits and require more time to graduate. Two-thirds are leaving college with large student loan debts. One in four who previously lived on his or her own is moving back with parents and one in eleven is unemployed. However, there is a mismatch between student aspirations and the economic realities they face. An overwhelming majority of undergraduates, a slightly higher percentage than in the 1990s, expect to be at least as well off financially as their parents.

This finding suggests that colleges and universities need to enrich their programs and services to better prepare students for today's economy and that government should invest a greater share of its resources in financial aid grants as well as providing a safety net for students with large financial aid burdens and limited job prospects.

In Contrast to Their Predecessors, Today's College Students Are More Immature, Dependent, Coddled, and Entitled

This is a generation of students who have not been permitted to skin their knees, rely much more on their parents than their predecessors, and have fathers and mothers, often described as *helicopter parents*, who are more involved in their lives and college affairs than ever before. Parents, schools, colleges, and employers have major roles to play in reversing this situation.

Today's College Students Were Born into and Will Live Their Lives in a Nation Enduring Unrelenting and Profound Change at a Speed and Magnitude Never Before Experienced

The United States is undergoing the third of the great revolutions in human history: the agricultural revolution, the industrial revolution, and whatever historians choose to name the transformation we are living through today. For the United States, this has been a time of dramatic demographic, economic, technological, and global change, which has in a very few years substantially altered many aspects of our lives from how we are conceived to when we die and seemingly everything in between—from how we communicate, entertain ourselves, and shop to how we date, bank, and work. It is a world in which all of our social institutions—government, media, health care, business, and education—appear to be broken. They were created for a different time and no longer function as well as they once did or as well as we need them to. They need to be remade for a new age. This is also a time when much that Americans took for granted is no longer true. Most Americans assumed their jobs, salaries, pensions, homes, and retirements were secure. When they woke up in the morning, they expected there would be a Soviet Union, a life-and-death struggle between Communism and capitalism, and the morning newspaper. Today's college students have and will be living in a time of constant change. The implication of this finding is that schools and colleges need to educate these students in the skills and knowledge essential for such an era, which might be called the three C's: critical thinking, creativity, and continual learning. This book suggests how this might be accomplished.

Current Undergraduates Grew up in a World Dramatically Different Than Their Parents

The parents of today's college students grew up in an analog, national, industrial society and their children grew up in a global, digital, information economy. The parents came of age in a world bereft of digital devices whereas their children were born after the advent of Apple, Microsoft, personal computers, CD's, mobile phones, e-mail, instant messaging, and the Internet. The parents grew up in an era of two superpowers and the threat of nuclear war and their children grew up on a flattening planet of weaker nation states and the promise of terrorism. As youngsters, the parents lived in an urban, white, more liberal country with its population concentrated in the Midwest and Northeast and their children came of age in a diverse, more conservative, suburban nation with a swelling immigrant population, concentrated in the South and West. This generation gap affects every institution and every adult who touches the lives of today's college students.

The Pace and Scale of Change Will Accelerate for the Nation and Its College Students

America's transition from an analog, national, industrial economy to a mature global, digital, information economy is not something that has occurred or will occur in two generations, no matter how different current undergraduates are from the adults in their lives. In the United States, the industrial revolution from launch to maturity was a six-generation process. The current revolution is likely to be shorter in duration if for no other reason than that the length of a generation has increased between revolutions and also because the speed of change is so much faster today. Nonetheless, the United States would have to be considered to be in the early stages, the infancy of the revolution, what might be called *global, digital, information economy 1.0.*

If the industrial revolution is any guide, the most profound changes occurred in the second half of the revolution—when water and steam power yielded to petroleum and electricity; when wood, stone, and iron gave way to steel; when railroads criss-crossed the country and telegraph and telephone lines knitted America into a nation; when the oil well, lightbulb, mass production steel mill, and assembly line were created; and when the great metropolises boomed and the modern corporation, bank, factory, and public regulatory system were established.

Today's college students will live their adult lives during the next stage in the development and flowering of the global, digital, information economy, the 2.0 world and beyond. Theirs will be a world that grows continually flatter; experiences new applications of existing technologies and a burgeoning of new technologies—nanotechnology, biotechnology, robotics, cognitive science, artificial intelligence, and infotechnology—and creates the mature information economy. All of these things are question marks for us today. We do not know what a flat world or a mature information economy looks like. We don't know what impact new technologies will have. And the greatest limitation of all is that we don't know what we don't know.

But here is what we do know. Today's college students will not only need to learn to live successfully in a world hurtling between its 1.0 and 2.0 versions but they also will have to create it.

Today's college students arrive on campus poorly prepared for this world, lacking in skills, knowledge, and attitudes that it will require though they bring strengths their predecessors lacked. Today's college students will need a very different education than the undergraduates who came before them, an education that prepares them for the twenty-first century. The colleges and universities that educate them are ill-equipped to offer that education today and will have to make major changes to provide it.

We also know that our own future depends on how well today's college students are prepared to meet the challenges ahead—living as engaged citizens in an evolving information economy, a diverse global society, and a digital age in a time of profound and relentless change. Therefore, this portrait of a generation also suggests specific ways we can better shape and collaborate with the next generation, who will then change the future.

June 2012   Arthur Levine
                                                              Princeton, New Jersey

                                                                 Diane R. Dean
                                                                 Normal, Illinois

ACKNOWLEDGMENTS

THE RESEARCH for this book spanned the years 2006 through 2011. Neither the research nor the book would have been possible without the help of thousands of people. We are grateful to every one of them—beginning with the senior student affairs officers and students who responded to our surveys and allowed us interview them. We wish to thank the Lumina Foundation for funding this project. Though its grant supported only this book, the Lumina project actually produced two books. This book was to focus not only on the students attending college but also the missing persons, the underrepresented populations who should be attending higher education but have been denied the opportunity. The study of missing persons resulted instead in a second book, *Unequal Fortunes: Snapshots from the Bronx* (Levine & Scheiber, 2010).

We are also grateful to the Rockefeller Foundation for providing a residency at their Bellagio Center to write this book. Without the support of the Lumina and Rockefeller Foundations, this book could not have been written. Leah Austin, Jill Kramer, Dewayne Matthews, and Holly Zanville at Lumina and Rob Garris, Pilar Palacia, and Elena Ogania of the Rockefeller Foundation were particularly important to us.

This project began at Teachers College, where Arthur and Diane worked. There we received the invaluable assistance of Jacquie Spano and Scott Fahey. Shortly after the project began, Diane, who served as principal investigator, moved to Illinois

State University. A year later, Arthur went to the Woodrow Wilson National Fellowship Foundation, where he was blessed to work with Carolyne Marrow, who coordinated the activities between Normal and Princeton, which had to be considered hardship duty.

We are thankful for the time and expertise of Phyllis McClusky-Titus, Helen Mamarchev, John Davenport, and Rick Olshak, who assisted us with the development of the senior student affairs officer and undergraduate student surveys; Carol Pfoff and Diana Weekes, who devoted late hours to work on the first wave of survey administration; and to Stacy Otto for her championship efforts and superhuman hours to assist with the second wave. We thank Rachel Levine for administering and overseeing the 2011 Student Affairs Survey.

Elizabeth Lugg, Wendy Troxel, Diane Wood, and Peter Richie teamed with us to conduct many campus visits and interviews. Grace Brown, Elizabeth Foste, John Giglio, Andrea Rediger, and Jackie Snelling transcribed the hundreds of hours of interviews. Carol Pfoff, Linda Wall, and Diana Weekes coordinated these activities. They have our very deep appreciation for very large contributions to this project.

We extend a thank-you to students at Allegheny College and Illinois State University who field tested and critiqued our undergraduate survey before we sent it out. We owe particular thanks to Rachel Levine, Katie O'Neill, Bryan Scheutz, and Mark Smeltz. We are indebted to each of the senior student affairs officers and staff at thirty-one colleges and universities, who tested our surveys, completed our surveys, and served as campus liaisons for day-long site visits to their campuses. They did an extraordinary amount of work, which made this research possible. Their names are listed in Appendix C.

We are also grateful to Howard Gardner, Margaret Weigel, and their colleagues at Project Zero for their generous collaboration.

We also thank Mary Callahan, Pat Callan, Gwen Dungy, Mike Usdan, and Ron Wolk for reading our manuscript and providing us with wise counsel on how to strengthen it. This book is much better because of their insights. We cannot overstate Shep Ranbom's contributions as counselor, friend, and muse.

David Brightman and Erin Null of Jossey-Bass have our gratitude for their patience and encouragement.

Above all the people who deserve the most gratitude are our families. Diane's husband, John Giglio, graciously tolerated the study's domination of his wife's life for years through the planning, long field work, surveys, and analysis. He listened and encouraged throughout the project. Arthur's wife, Linda Fentiman, was a wise counselor. She, too, listened endlessly, advised when asked, consoled and encouraged when needed, and chided when necessary.

ARTHUR LEVINE is the sixth president of the Woodrow Wilson National Fellowship Foundation (2006–present). Before his appointment at Woodrow Wilson, he was president and professor of education at Teachers College, Columbia University (1994–2006). He also previously served as a faculty member and chair of the Institute for Educational Management at the Harvard Graduate School of Education (1989–1994), president of Bradford College (1982–1989), and senior fellow at the Carnegie Foundation for the Advancement of Teaching and Carnegie Council on Policy Studies in Higher Education (1975–1982).

Dr. Levine is the author of scores of articles, which have appeared in such publications as the *New York Times*, the *Los Angeles Times*, the *Wall Street Journal*, and the *Washington Post*. He has also authored, coauthored, or edited eleven books, the most recent of which is *Unequal Fortunes: Snapshots from the Bronx* (with Laura Scheiber).

Dr. Levine has received a number of honors, including a Guggenheim Fellowship, membership in the American Academy of Arts and Sciences, and twenty four honorary degrees.

Dr. Levine received his bachelor's degree from Brandeis University and his PhD from the State University of New York at Buffalo.

DIANE R. DEAN is associate professor of higher education administration and policy at Illinois State University and principal investigator of the Portrait of Today's College Student study. Dr. Dean's research and publications focus on leadership, governance, and organizational issues in colleges and universities; higher education policy and its formation; the careers, work experiences and cultures of college and university faculty and academic administrators; and the sociocultural and classroom experiences of undergraduate students.

Dean is coeditor of the *Women in Academe* series (with Jeanie Allen and Susan Bracken), which examines gendered issues among students, faculty, and academic leadership; and coeditor of *Public Policy and Higher Education* (with Cheryl Lovell, Toni Larson, and David Longnecker). Dean received her bachelor's degree from the University of Maryland, College Park, and her master's and doctorate from Teachers College, Columbia University.

Generation on a Tightrope

Introduction

THIS BOOK PRESENTS a snapshot of US undergraduates enrolled in college between 2005 through 2014. It is the third book in an unintended trilogy. Arthur Levine is a product of the late 1960s. That's when Arthur went to college. The first book in the trilogy, *When Dreams and Heroes Died* (Levine, 1980), was a study carried out for the Carnegie Council on Policy Studies in Higher Education that compared the undergraduates of the Jimmy Carter era with the students of Arthur's day. Like its successors, this book was the result of surveys of nationally representative samples of undergraduates and senior student affairs officers as well information gathered from site visits to more than two dozen college and university campuses, chosen to represent the diversity of US higher education. During the visits interviews were conducted with the senior student affairs officer, student government president, student newspaper editor, and a focus group of diverse students. The details of these data sources are discussed in Appendix B.

The first book described a self-concerned, pragmatic, and social generation of undergraduates who were optimistic about their personal futures and deeply concerned about material and career success but pessimistic about the country's future. They were liberal on social issues, moderate in politics, disenchanted with government, and lacking in heroes. A second book was not anticipated.

The second book, *When Hope and Fear Collide* (Levine & Cureton, 1998), was a result of continuing conversations with undergraduates when visiting campuses for other purposes. For years, the students gave roughly the same answers to the same questions as their predecessors had in the first study. Then, very quickly, seemingly overnight, their answers changed rather dramatically. For instance, in contrast to the students of the 1970s undergraduates said they had heroes and had become more active politically, focusing on local issues. That caused Arthur, who was joined by Jeanette Cureton, to carry out a second study to try to learn what had happened and why.

The second book painted a picture of a generation that described itself as *tired*, torn between hope and fear of the future and committed to preserving the American Dream. They were more optimistic than their predecessors; had heroes, most often their parents; retreated from organized politics; and were issue oriented rather than ideological. They were actively involved in community service and their focus was local. With deep divisions by race, they were socially isolated and sexually engaged, more pragmatic than romantic.

This third book began with a mistake. The previous studies asked college students what social or political events had the greatest impact on them and their generation. The students of the 1970s answered Watergate, Vietnam, and the civil rights movement. The students of the 1990s did not have a common event. Their answers, which differed by race and gender, included the 1991 Gulf War, the explosion of the space shuttle *Challenger*, the fall of the Berlin Wall, the Exxon Valdez Alaskan oil spill, the excessive force trial of Los Angeles police officers who arrested Rodney King, the collapse of the Soviet Union, and the AIDS epidemic. In contrast to the students of the 1970s, they said the events did not have a significant impact on their lives.

It seemed to us that the terrorist attacks of September 11, 2001, and the events that followed in its aftermath would be the signal events for current undergraduates, as powerful as the Depression or World War II in giving shape to a generation. This would be the September 11 generation. We undertook this study to find out who this generation was and to understand the effects of the terrorist bombing on young people.

The only shortcoming in the plan was that students said September 11 was not the key event in their lives. Rather, it was the establishment of the World Wide Web. Of importance, but to a lesser degree, were the election of Barack Obama, the world financial crisis, and September 11. Although this was a shock to us, it should not have been. The Internet has affected seemingly every aspect of collegiate life from the classroom and personal relationships to student politics and entertainment. We are convinced that the changes we are witnessing today are only the beginning of a cascade that will follow, touching not only current undergraduates but also transforming the world of their successors: the colleges, universities, and institutions and the people who surround them.

A lot has changed since the first book was published; actually an amazing amount has changed. At the time *When Dreams and Heroes Died* was published, there were no DVDs, CDs, Kindles, iPods, iPads, or iPhones; no texting, tweeting, skyping, or IMing. Mark Zuckerberg, LeBron James, Britney Spears, and Paris Hilton had not yet been born. Barack Obama was a teenager and Osama bin Laden had just left college. There were no companies named Amazon, Facebook, eBay, Dell Computer, or Whole Foods Markets. *The Cosby Show, Friends, The Simpsons, Seinfeld,* and *Cheers* were not yet on television; *E.T.* and *Raiders of the Lost Ark* had not yet been released; and Cabbage Patch Kids, Teenage Mutant Ninja Turtles, American Girl dolls, and Transformers had not yet appeared either. (If instead of writing *Dreams and Heroes,* Arthur had invested in almost any of these things, he would be very wealthy today.) The United States was waging the Cold War and the Mujahideen in Afghanistan were our allies. The Soviet

Union, East Germany, Yugoslavia, and Czechoslovakia still existed; Nelson Mandela was in prison; Jimmy Carter was president; and CNN was just founded.

The students portrayed in this book grew up in a dramatically different world than the undergraduates described in the two previous books. The temptation is to give them a name to signify how they are different. In the United States, we like to name college generations. By way of definition, a generation, for those who are interested, can refer either to students who are the same age or share common historical events or experiences. The definitions overlap a good deal and both are used in this book.

We have names and images for every generation of college students based on their fads, foibles, and circumstances; the ways in which they seem most different from the undergraduates who came before them. So, the students of the Roaring Twenties, who will be forever remembered in raccoon coats and flapper dresses, drinking from hip flasks, and dancing the Charleston, were called the *lost generation*. Their counterparts of the 1930s, named the *Depression generation*, were out of work and out of luck. The 1940s and 1950s brought the *silent generation*, wearing gray flannel suits and eagerly and compliantly seeking to rebuild lives interrupted by World War II. Then came the 1960s *baby boomers*, the generation of sex, drugs, rock and roll, and protest, who sported bell bottom jeans, tie-dyed T-shirts, and love beads. The students of the late 1970s and 1980s were the *me generation*, conservative, well coiffed, well dressed, and seeking to be well off. They were followed in the 1990s by *generation X*, who were actually anointed with an assortment of different labels: *twenty-somethings, slackers, the thirteenth generation,* and *baby busters*, among others, because they defied easy classification.

With each newly perceived generation of college students, there is what can only be described as a contest or race to name them. The way it works is that contestants write, film, or record an article, video, or song with a name for the generation and see if it sticks. The winners with the stickiest names receive spectacular prizes, including media attention, speaking fees, consulting opportunities, and endorsement possibilities.

With current students, as with their predecessors, the various entrees in the current name-that-generation contest focus on different aspects of their being, some more imaginatively than others. Current undergraduates have been called *millennials* (Howe & Strauss, 1992) and *generation 2K* (Zoba, 1999) because they are a part of the first college generation of the twenty-first century. They have also been called *generation Y* (Tulgan, 2009) and *generation iY* (Elmore & Cathy, 2010), which is logical because they followed generation X and are partial to the Internet. There is *generation Z* (Hopkins, 2005) because they are the children of generation X. Building on that Internet theme are the meat and potatoes *Internet generation* (Milner, 2010), the too-easy-to-confuse-with-basketball *net generation* (Tapscott, 2008), the insightful *digital natives* (Palfrey & Gasser, 2010), and the less committal *digital generation* (Jukes, 2010). There must be an *iGeneration* somewhere but we haven't found it. Taking an entirely different tack are the names *me-first generation* (Lipkin, 2009), meaning they are a tad self-involved, and *echo-boom generation* (Alch, 2000), referring to the fact that these are the children of the baby boomers, not booming like their parents, just echoing. And so it goes.

As of this writing *millennials* leads the pack in popularity with *generation Y* following second but seeming to have faded because it may or may not refer to a somewhat older group of young people. The problem is that different authors sometimes ascribe different birth years to generations, often when using the same cohort name. In any case, google *millennial generation* and you will find there are 824,000 listings. Search Amazon.com and you'll find more than one thousand books—hardcovers, paperbacks, Kindle editions, HTML, and audiobooks. (In the interest of candor, it should be noted that the one thousand number is somewhat inflated because for some of the titles, there are separate listings for the hardcover, paperback, audio, and Kindle editions.) These books cover an amazing array of subjects, ranging from gay millennials (Boone, 2000) and Christian millennials (Miller, 2003) to millennials as employees (Lancaster, 2010), political forces (Winograd & Hais, 2009), students (McHaney & Daniel, 2011), children (Vanderhaagen, 2005), and members of a global and multicultural society (Dolby, 2012). There is a paucity of self-help books, though.

The student newspaper editor at Swarthmore explained her objection to the practice of naming generations and to the name *millennials* in particular. She attended a lecture by a fellow who "labeled my generation as *millennials* and it really pissed me off . . . This guy assumed he knew everything about me when he really didn't know anything about me."

It is easy and perhaps unfair to poke fun at these efforts to describe generations. The problem is that the names describe only a facet of a generation, not the whole. In this sense, they conceal more than they reveal. College student attitudes, values, and experiences are continually shifting and changing. For the most part, these changes are matters of degree rather than kind. Generational names focus on the most visible of the changes. With time, however, the stereotype becomes more real than the generation itself. The students devolve into caricatures that eclipse the very real diversity found in every generation.

As described in the previous books, a good example, because the data exist to contrast image and reality, is the college student of the 1960s. In general, this generation was not political. In 1969, near the height of college student protests, less than a third of all undergraduates (28 percent) had participated in a demonstration (Gallup International, 1969). In May 1970, during the week of the most widespread student protests in US history following the

killings of students at Kent and Jackson state universities, 43 percent
of the nation's colleges and universities were entirely unaffected
(Peterson, 1971). Moreover, student political attitudes in the
1960s were decidedly middle-of-the road or conservative; only a
third of undergraduates in 1969 described themselves as liberal or
left of center (Undergraduate Survey, 1969). Most undergraduates
(59 percent) came to college for the reason students have come to
college for a thousand years—to get training and skills for an occupation (Undergraduate Survey, 1969). Nearly half (49 percent) saw
the chief benefit of a college education as increasing their earning
power (Undergraduate Survey, 1969).[1]

This book seeks to paint a multifaceted portrait of the most
diverse generation of college students ever to arrive on campus by
including their hopes and aspirations, beliefs and values, academic
experience, life beyond the classroom, politics, relationships, use
of technology, and historic context. The book examines what
has changed, what has shifted, and what remains the same about
today's students. It discusses the future this generation faces and
the roles of parents, colleges, employers, and government in preparing them for that future.

Chapter One discusses the differences in the worlds in
which today's college students and the adults in their lives grew
up and four events that helped to shape this generation of college students: the advent of the World Wide Web and the other
digital technologies that followed, the worldwide recession, the
September 11 terrorist attack and its aftermath, and the election
of Barack Obama.

The second chapter focuses on academics, describing a generation living through an economic downturn that is more career
oriented and pragmatic, more satisfied with college and their professors, and more likely to engage in plagiarism, disrupt classes,
and have inflated grades than their predecessors. They want more
technology in the curriculum.

The next chapter examines social life on and off campus, discussing the decreasing participation of students in campus activities, what students do for fun (drinking, partying, and sex), the impact of digital technology on social life, and the rise of what we call *the new tribalism*, digital communities unique to each student.

The fourth chapter focuses on the growing involvement of parents in their children's lives. It highlights the increasing frequency of contact between parents and their offspring and the rising involvement of parents in college life.

Chapter Five reports on the changing multicultural climate on campus, finding diverse groups of undergraduates are more satisfied with college, have less polarized views, and believe progress is being made on issues of race, ethnicity, and gender. Across groups students share more common life experiences, and within groups there is greater diversity of life experiences. Interaction among students of different races and ethnicities has increased.

Politics on and off campus is the subject of Chapter Six. It describes an issue-oriented, engaged generation of students with less interest in college governance and campus activism than their predecessors. They are instead more concerned with issues beyond the college gates—talking globally but acting locally.

The seventh chapter deals with student views of the future. This is a generation optimistic about their personal futures and pessimistic about the future of the country but still showing a commitment to the American Dream and higher aspirations for material and personal success than their predecessors.

The final chapter focuses on the world in which current college students will live their lives and the demands it will make on them. It reviews from the previous chapters the attributes students bring to college today and finds they are ill-prepared for the future that awaits them. It discusses the education necessary to prepare today's students for that world and reports that it will necessitate major changes on the part of the nation's colleges and universities.

The chapter concludes with an examination of the challenges and opportunities this generation poses for employers, parents, and government.

This book focuses principally on traditional college students, eighteen to twenty-five years of age and attending college largely full time. The distinction between traditional and nontraditional students has blurred a bit in recent years because students are working longer hours and taking fewer credits because of the recession and the rising costs of college. However, traditional students differ profoundly from their older peers, who are more often working, female, attending college part time, and juggling a host of responsibilities—families, spouses, jobs, friends, and college. Often college is not the principal priority in their lives, being overshadowed by family and jobs.

Their relationship with college is much like the relationships they have with all the other service providers in their lives—the bank, the phone and Internet and television companies, and the supermarket. They are looking for the same four things from each of them: convenience, service, quality, and low prices.

For higher education, this means nontraditional students want the college to be conveniently located, parking to be available near classrooms, courses to be offered when they need to take them, and classes and office hours at convenient times. They are looking for good customer services from admissions, financial aid, and registrars who are committed to helping students. They want high-quality instruction relevant to the real world with up-to-date professors who know how to teach and return assignments and tests quickly with comments. And they want low tuitions and fees. They are willing to shop around, though a goodly number have more money than time.

They do not want to pay for what they are not using. This is a group that tends to come to campus just for classes—ride in, ride out. They do not want to pay for the athletic center they are not using, the elective courses they are not taking, or the student activities they aren't attending. They are asking for a stripped down version of higher education.

They are markedly different from traditional students who are asking for collegiate life with all the bells and whistles. Nontraditional students have different relationships and expectations for their colleges. They use their colleges differently. They engage in different activities. They ask more and less of their colleges and are if anything more consumer oriented.

A word on citations is necessary. Four student surveys are cited in this book: the 1969, 1976, 1993, and 2009 Undergraduate Surveys. There were also five senior student affairs officer surveys, which are cited as Student Affairs Survey 1978, 1992, 1997, 2008, and 2011. We promised interviewees we would not use their names. The terms *senior student affairs officer, dean of students, vice president for student affairs*, and *vice chancellor for student affairs* are used interchangeably.

Note

1. This paragraph is taken almost verbatim from *When Hope and Fear Collide* (Levine & Cureton, 1998, p. 2).

1

The Past Is a Foreign Country

The past is a foreign country.
They do things differently there.
—HARTLEY (1953)

THIS IS a portrait of the students who attended college between 2005 and 2014. They grew up at a time of profound, swift, continuing, and disruptive economic, demographic, technological, and global change and have lived their lives in a very different world than their parents. The world of their parents and professors was dying and their world was being born simultaneously.

This generation faces a situation reminiscent of an optical illusion commonly found in books of children's brain teasers and introductory psychology textbooks called *faces and vases*. It is a black-and-white picture in which one can see either two faces or a vase, never both at the same time. The faces are black and the vase is white. If one sees the white as background and the black as foreground, two faces appear on the left and right sides of the picture with a white space separating them. If one views the black as background and the white as foreground, a vase appears at the center of a picture bordered in black. The worlds of today's college students and their parents exist in a similar fashion. For each, the world they grew up in is foreground. For adults there is an increasing realization that their world is receding into the background, often accompanied by a sense of loss, and that their children's world is emerging in the foreground. The parents have begun to live their lives straddling both worlds. Their children have less appreciation for what is happening; their parents' world was never foreground. It never existed for them.

The Worlds of the Class of 2012 and Their Parents

America's traditional undergraduates, represented by the class of 2012, were born in 1990.[1] A chronology of the major events in their lifetime can be found in Appendix A. Technologically, the parents of the class of 2012 are products of an analog world and their children grew up in a digital age, using a numerical rather than wave technology, which is cheaper, faster, more reliable, more accurate, and more productive. Apple, Microsoft, and AOL already existed when the class of 2012 was born. There were already personal computers, CDs, mobile phones, e-mail, instant messaging, and the Internet. By the time they were in kindergarten, texting, web browsers, smart phones, DVDs, Yahoo!, and the dot-com bubble were realities. Before they finished elementary school, Google, Napster, music file sharing, and the iPod had come onto the scene. Middle school brought Skype, Myspace, and Facebook. They had to wait until high school for YouTube, Twitter, and the iPhone.

Globally, the parents of the class of 2012 grew up in a time of nation states with two superpowers and a cold war. Their children were born into a world that was flattening as Thomas Friedman would proclaim when they were fifteen years old (Friedman, 2005). By the time the class of 2012 was three years old, the old world order was collapsing. The Cold War, Soviet Union, and Berlin Wall were gone. The countries of East Germany, Yugoslavia, and Czechoslovakia had ceased to exist. The Maastricht Treaty, creating a European Union, had been signed. There was no Red China; the United States and China had normalized relations. A Muslim state had been established in Iran and the State of Palestine had been created. The Arab-Israeli conflict and initiatives to end it had been going on for four decades.

In contrast to their parents, the class of 2012 grew up in a global society, bounded together by the movement of information, money, jobs, trade, investment, and business, facing many common challenges. The United States was inextricably intertwined to that world. The independence of nation states was waning and national borders were becoming increasingly porous. The degree to which this was true was demonstrated vividly by the worldwide recession when class of 2012 turned eighteen.

The changes in the world caused different dangers and fears for parents and children. The parents grew up with the persistent threat of nuclear war by nation states. Their children lived with the reality of insurgent terrorism at home, carried out by networks rather than nations, fighting globalization and the fear that these organizations might detonate weapons of mass destruction in the United States. Before today's college students were born, their parents witnessed terrorism abroad, targeted at Americans. But their children saw terrorism come to the United States. When they were three, terrorists attempted to blow up the World Trade Center. Two years later, Americans carried out the then-worst terrorist attack in US history, bombing the Oklahoma City federal building, killing 168 people and injuring 450. The next terrorist attack was larger and more horrible. When they were eleven, terrorists belonging to al-Qaeda flew jumbo jets into the World Trade Center and the Pentagon, killing nearly three thousand people. They watched it again and again and again on television—the planes hitting the towers and the towers collapsing. Later, there were headlines trumpeting terrorist attacks in Madrid, London, Mumbai, and around the globe, continually reminding them of what might happen again at home. They heard accounts of failed terrorist attacks including a shoe bombing on a Detroit-bound plane and a car bombing in New York City's Times Square. They also witnessed another form of domestic terrorism in which students massacred fellow students at Columbine High School in Colorado when they were ten and at Virginia Tech seven years later. The United States has been at war since they were eleven years old for reasons ascribed to terrorism.

Economically, the parents of the class of 2012 were the products of an industrial society that was shifting to an information economy whereas their children grew up in an information economy still transitioning from the industrial society. By the time this generation of college students was born, jobs in the manufacturing sector were declining and moving abroad. The historic manufacturing regions of the United States were commonly called the *rust belt*, a term popularized in the 1980s. There was already little economic future for high school dropouts. The jobs that paid salaries adequate to support a family required more education and greater knowledge and skills than ever before. High-paying jobs, demanding high levels of education, were on a steep rise.

Demographically, the class of 2012 grew up in a nation that was populated differently than their parents. In 1960, when many of their parents were born or soon would be, a majority of Americans lived in the Northeast and Midwest (56 percent). By the time the class of 2012 was born, the numbers had flip-flopped—55 percent lived in the South and West and the disparity continued to grow. The impact of the change is that parents came of age at time in which the United States was dominated by blue (and liberal Republican) states and their children grew up in an era in which the balance of power shifted to the red states (Gibson & Jung, 2002).

The US population aged between the parents' and children's generations. In 1960, slightly more than one out of eight Americans (13 percent) was over the age of sixty. In 2010, the proportion rose to nearly one in five (18 percent). By 2050, when the class of 2012 turns sixty, the numbers are projected to grow to one in four (26 percent). The result is that today's college students are facing a mounting financial burden for their parents' and grandparents' Social Security, Medicare, and other senior programs and the likelihood that these programs will be significantly changed by the time they are eligible for them (US Administration on Aging, 2008).

Current students live in a society in which immigration has reached the highest numbers in modern history, more than three times the rate their parents experienced growing up. During the 1960s, 3.2 million immigrants entered the country as legal residents. During the 1990s, the number jumped to 9.8 million and in the first decade of the twenty-first century it reached more than a million a year—10.3 million. The makeup of the immigrant population changed dramatically as well. In the 1960s, 35 percent of the immigrants came from Europe, 11 percent from Asia, and 21 percent from Latin America. Between 1990 and 2009, Europeans dropped by nearly two-thirds (13 percent) whereas Hispanics more than doubled (45 percent) and Asians tripled (32 percent) (Office of Immigration Statistics, 2011).

One of the consequences of legal and illegal immigration as well as varying fertility rates of different ethnic groups is that the class of 2012 lives in a far more diverse society than their parents. In fact, they are the most diverse college generation in US history. In 1960, 85 percent of the nation's population was white, 12 percent was black, 4 percent was Hispanic, and 1 percent was Asian. In 2010, the proportion of non-Hispanic whites dropped by a quarter (65 percent), blacks remained constant (13 percent), Hispanics quadrupled (16 percent), and Asians quintupled (5 percent). By

2050, whites are projected to make up a minority of the population (46 percent) in a nation in which Hispanics (30 percent), blacks (13 percent), and Asians (8 percent) constitute the new majority (Humes, 2011; US Census Bureau, 2002).

The parents of the class of 2012 were born into an America that had anti-miscegenation laws in sixteen states until 1967. In contrast, their children are living in a country in which 5.6 percent of children under the age of eighteen are multiracial (Mather, 2011).

With these changes, the class of 2012 watched as racial and gender ceilings cracked. Blacks and women had run for president and vice president before the class of 2012 was born. Women and people of color had served in legislatures, statehouses, and city halls. After the class of 2012 was born, they made further advances. When the class of 2012 was seventeen, the first woman was elected speaker of the US House of Representatives. A year later, a black-skinned, multiracial man was elected president of the United States; the Democratic nomination for president came down to a white woman and a black man and the Republican Party nominated its first female vice-presidential candidate. The year after that a Latina was appointed to the US Supreme Court.

In contrast to their parents, today's college students are a more diverse, digital generation living in an information economy with an aging, increasingly immigrant, migrating population, a majority of whom reside in the South and West. Their world is flat, financially troubled, and inflamed by religious, economic, and political differences. See Table 1.1 for a description of today's college students and their parents.

In *When Hope and Fear Collide*, the college students of the 1990s were described as a transitional generation, with one foot in the world of their parents and the other in the world being born. In contrast, the students of the twenty-first century have both feet in the new world, with an important caveat: their parents' generation is still largely in control of the nation's social

Table 1.1   Today's College Students and Their Parents

	Parents	*Students*
Technology	Analog	Digital
Globe	Dominated by nation states with two superpowers and a cold war	Flat with weaker nation states and terrorist opponents
Economy	Industrial economy transitioning to an information economy	Information economy transitioning from an industrial economy
Demographics	White, majority of population in Northeast and Midwest with middle-aged baby boomers	Diverse with majority of population in the West and South, aging baby boomers, and increased immigration

institutions—government, health care, education, finance, and to a lesser extent media.

In that book, the story of Rip Van Winkle was used as metaphor for the extraordinary pace of change our society was experiencing, that in a very short period of time an overwhelming amount of change can occur. That story also gives insight into the generational differences we are experiencing today. Washington Irving's 1819 tale is the story of a man who sleeps for twenty years and wakes up believing he's slept a single night. He walks through the village where he lives and not surprisingly does not recognize the homes, businesses, names on the doors, or the people he sees. Shocked, nearly mad, Rip Van Winkle cries out, "Everything's changed and I'm changed and I can't tell what's my name, or who I am" (Irving, 2011, line 242).

The story could have been told from a very different perspective, albeit a far less interesting one: from the point of view of the people who lived in the village. They would report that one day, an elderly man with an old-fashioned gun, unlike any the young people had seen before, and clothing from back in the day, more appropriate to a costume party than a stroll through the village, appeared in town. He told an absurd story, claiming he lived in this village, though no one recognized him including the people who were his children. He was pitiful. They felt sorry for him and allowed him to stay. With time, acceptance grew to affection, though the old man remained a curiosity who continued to tell every stranger who passed through the village about the old days. As the years passed, he came to comprehend the changes that occurred while he slept, but only as one who has heard a story rather than living it.

In the first version, Rip Van Winkle is the native and the village is the stranger, shocking and incomprehensible. In the second, the village is the native and Rip Van Winkle is the stranger, old, disconnected, and out of touch. In many respects, this is our situation today. Many of us adults are Rip Van Winkles, natives of a dying world and immigrants in an emerging world. Our children are the natives of the new world and immigrants in the old, to the extent that they are aware of it. In his autobiography, Henry Adams offered this account of his own world, shifting from an agrarian to an industrial society, referring to himself in the third person:

> The old universe was thrown in the ash-heap and a new one was created. . . . [Adams] and his eighteenth-century troglodytic Boston were cut apart—separated forever— not in sentiment, but by the opening of the Boston and Albany Railroad; the appearance of the first Cunard steamers in the bay and the telegraphic messages which carried from Baltimore to Washington the news that Henry Clay and James K. Polk were nominated for president (Adams, lines 17405 ff).

Key Events in the Lives of Today's College Students

Events define generations. There are occasions, happenings, circumstances, and shared experiences of such importance that they exert a formative impact on the young people who live through them. For example, the undergraduates of the 1930s might have said the Depression was such an event. The students of the 1940s might have selected World War II. When surveyed in the late 1970s, undergraduates chose Watergate, Vietnam, and the civil rights movement (Levine, 1980). The students of the 1990s identified an array of events that were significant but of lesser impact to their generation: the Persian Gulf War, the explosion of the space shuttle *Challenger*, the fall of the Berlin Wall, the Exxon Valdez oil spill, the Rodney King trial of police officers for using excessive force, the breakup of the Soviet Union, and the AIDS epidemic (Levine & Cureton, 1998).

In the 2009 academic year, we asked undergraduates about the key events that shaped their lives. We did this first in campus focus groups to learn the answers students would give and then we surveyed a nationally representative sample of college students (Undergraduate Survey, 2009). We gave them a list of fifty-two events, some occurring before they were born, most after, and asked how important they were to them, on a four-point scale ranging from a low of "not significant" to a high of "key event" in my life.

The events they rated as key are the advent of the World Wide Web and digital technologies that followed, the worldwide economic recession, the September 11 attack and its aftermath, and the election of Barack Obama as president. In a number of ways, these events reflect the differences between college students and their parents—technologically (the advent of the World Wide Web), economically (the worldwide recession), globally

Table 1.2   Key Events in the Lives of Undergraduates

	Percent citing
Launch of World Wide Web	42
Economy (gas prices exceed $4 per gallon)	37
September 11 attack	29
Obama nomination and election	25
Mass use of cell phones	23
Launch of Yahoo!	20

Source: Undergraduate Survey (2009).

(September 11 and its aftermath), and demographically (the election of Barack Obama). Table 1.2 lists the six events cited by at least 20 percent of the students surveyed.

Technology

This is the first generation of digital natives to attend college. Three of the top six events they cited were new technologies: the World Wide Web, cell phone, and Yahoo! They rated the launch of the World Wide Web as the key event in their lives. Nearly three-quarters (74 percent) said it was either very important or key to them (Undergraduate Survey, 2009).

When we asked college students how they adapted to the tidal wave of new technology, one explained, "It's only technology if it happened after you were born." (At the time, the comment seemed to us a confession of ignorance with the potential to someday grace the bumper of a car as opposed to a very wise observation.) If the technology exists before you were born, it's a fact of life, a given. The question would be the equivalent of asking their parents or professors how they adapted to the telephone, radio, or automobile. They didn't have to. These things were just there.

The speed of adoption of new media by this generation has been extraordinary. At the time of Undergraduate Survey, Facebook was four years old and Myspace was five. They would have to be considered relatively new technologies. Yet 85 percent of college students reported using them or other online social media. Half said they were using them one or more times daily and a quarter said one or more times a week for an average of nearly four and a half hours a week (Undergraduate Survey, 2009). We suspect those numbers would be much inflated today. The rapid adoption has to be put into context. The basics were already in place when this generation born or very young and many of the popular innovations represented changes in degree rather than kind, little more than the difference between the detergent Tide and new blue Tide.

Over and over students said, "It will definitely be technology that defines our generation. . . . It's what we have grown up with." "If you remove the computer, text messages, e-mail, cell phones, BlackBerries . . . I will probably die." They asked, "How did you live before?" On three different campuses, students reported giving up Facebook for Lent.

No change is larger or will have greater impact on higher education than this generation's use of digital technology. It is what differentiates current undergraduates from the students who came before them and separates them from the older adults on campus and at home. The reasons go far beyond the hardware and software they own, the applications they use, the websites they flock to, and the social media that have become nearly universal.

There are fundamental differences between today's undergraduates and their colleges, rooted in the new technologies. Digital technologies have made current college students a 24/7 generation, operating around the clock, any time, any place. However, they attend colleges with fixed locations and fixed calendars— semesters, course schedules, and office hours. How many of us have gotten e-mails at 3 AM from students who are annoyed when they do not receive a response within a few hours?

Digital technologies place an accent on learning and encourage group activity, shared work products, and consumer-driven content. But current undergraduates are enrolled in universities where the emphasis is on teaching, individual work products, and content is university or producer driven. How many of us have faced students who have committed plagiarism and, having grown up with file sharing, say they don't understand why it was wrong?

Digital technologies permit multitasking and individualized and interactive learning. The preferred content and modes of learning for students are concrete (practical) and active (hands on). But professors favor serial tasking, doing one task at a time, and passive (hands off, for example, reading) and abstract (theoretical) learning. How many of us have shaken our heads in dismay as we watched a student in a coffee shop sitting with a friend, talking on a cell phone with another person, and working on a class assignment and wondered why our students have so much trouble with Plato and Tolstoy?

Digital media produce a shallow ocean of information and encourage students to gather and sift. Of course, they can go deeper if they wish. But they matriculate into analog universities, populated by academics who are hunters, whose interests and work generally emphasizes depth over breadth. How many of us are still surprised when students cite *Wikipedia* as the primary source in papers and neglect to check even the most basic academic resources? See Table 1.3 for a contrast between the focus of traditional universities and this generation of digital students.

The impact of technology goes far beyond the classroom. It changes student communications and relationships with peers, parents, and colleges. One dean explained that his office no longer knew how to contact students living on campus. They either don't have or don't use room phones. They have cell phones. They

Table 1.3   Traditional Universities and Digital Students

Traditional Universities	Digital Natives
Fixed time (semesters, credits, office hours)	Variable time—24/7
Location bound	Any time, any place
Provider driven (university determined)	Consumer driven (student determined)
Passive learning (hands off)	Active learning (hands on)
Abstract	Concrete
Analog media	Digital media
Teaching (process)	Learning (outcome)
Individual	Group (collaborative)
Depth focus (hunting)	Breadth focus (gathering)

don't answer e-mail coming to their college accounts. They have several other accounts and often don't check those regularly, preferring to text. New technologies change the way students meet, entertain, protest, get their news, shop, participate in politics, spend their time, and use the campus. They change the rules for how people conduct their lives, establish new standards of decorum, and create new opportunities for incivility. Between 2008 and 2011, 46 percent of campuses surveyed reported increased levels of technology-based infractions and misbehavior and 44 percent had increases in technology-based incivility (Student Affairs Survey, 2011).

When the authors expressed surprise at the level at which college undergraduates use technology, students often remarked, "you should see my younger sister or brother." Among adults eighteen to thirty-four years old, 95 percent have cell phones, 74 percent have iPods or other MP3 players, 70 percent have laptop computers, 63 percent have game consoles, and 5 percent have iPads or other tablets. Only 1 percent had none of these devices.

No age group had a higher percentage in any of these categories (Pew Internet and American Life Project, 2011), except their younger brothers and sisters (ages twelve to seventeen), who have more iPods (79 percent) and game consoles (80 percent) (Pew Internet and American Life Project, 2011). They text more often (104 versus 62 daily) and have more personal blogs (60 percent versus 43 percent) (The Digital Future Project, 2011). These are the young people coming to college next.

The Economy

The first wave of surveys for the 2009 survey was sent out in October 2008. At that time, the dimension of the recession that would follow was still unclear, though momentous events had already occurred. International financial firms had written off more than $500 billion in assets in August and the International Monetary Fund predicted that the actual need was $1.5 trillion. In September, the US government took over Fannie Mae and Freddie Mac, Lehman Brothers failed, and Merrill Lynch was sold to Bank of America. On October 3, President Bush signed a $700 billion federal bailout bill.

The student survey included two economic issues—gas prices rising above $4 a gallon in July and the subprime mortgage crisis that began in 2007 but was only becoming apparent to the nation in fall 2008. Of the students surveyed 37 percent said increased gas prices was the key event in their lives and 9 percent selected the subprime mortgage crisis (Undergraduate Survey, 2009). Our conversations lead us to believe they were proxies for the troubled economy.

Students were living through a severe international recession that produced high unemployment, foreclosures, bankruptcies, increased national debt and oil prices, the loss of 8.5 million jobs, and declines in home prices, consumer confidence, international trade, and credit. The subprime mortgage crisis left major banks, insurance companies, and manufacturing firms teetering at the edge of bankruptcy, saved only by federal bailouts.

This is a generation that is highly critical of business. They overwhelmingly believe private corporations are too concerned with profits and not enough with public responsibility and CEOs do not deserve the high salaries they receive. This is discussed more fully in Chapter Six (Undergraduate Survey, 2009).

The recession has had a very large impact on whether, where, and how students attend college. Historically, college enrollments have grown when the economy is weak. Attendance hit record levels in 2009–2010, when 74 percent of female and 63 percent of male 2009 high school graduates enrolled and the jobless rate for high school graduates not enrolled in college rose to 33 percent. A year later when economic conditions improved slightly, enrollment rates dropped slightly (US Bureau of Labor Statistics, 2011).

The economy affected where students went to college. More than three out of five 2010–2011 college freshmen (62 percent) said the current economic situation affected where they went to college. Almost half (46 percent) chose their college because it offered financial assistance versus a third (34 percent) in 2006 before the recession began (Pryor, 2007; Pryor & DeAngelo, 2010).

The economy changed the way students attended college. Between 2008 and 2011, two-thirds of senior student affairs officers (67 percent) surveyed reported increases in the number of students at their universities who were working longer hours. A quarter or more said students were stopping out (taking a hiatus from college with the intent of returning) (48 percent), living at home (48 percent), choosing or changing majors (36 percent), dropping out (33 percent), and taking fewer credits (31 percent) because of the economy (see Table 1.4) (Student Affairs Survey, 2011).

In 2009, 69 percent of all college students surveyed were working at paid jobs, up from 60 percent in 1993 and 54 percent in 1976. Almost half (46 percent) of those with jobs were working

Table 1.4　**Impact of the Economy on Students by Percent of Institutions**

	Increased	Remained the Same	Decreased
Working longer hours due to the economy	67	33	
Living at home due to the economy	48	48	4
Stopping out due to the economy	48	41	11
Dropping out due to the economy	33	51	11
Taking fewer credits due to the economy	31	58	12
Choosing or changing majors due to the economy	36	64	

Source: Student Affairs Survey (2011).

twenty-one hours a week or more. When asked the primary reason they were working, 16 percent said they wanted money to help pay tuition or basic living expenses and 64 percent said they needed the money for that purpose (Undergraduate Survey, 2009). In 2010, full-time students were half as likely to be working as their part-time peers (US Bureau of Labor Statistics, 2011).

Student affairs officers described their students as more stressed and anxious, more academically driven, more frequently using psychological counseling services, and in a hurry to finish college. They were also more career focused, spent more time in the career counseling office, and were eager for internships, particularly paid ones or anything else that would give them an edge in the job market (Student Affairs Survey, 2011).

Their greatest immediate concern was money. Family circumstances have changed. Of college students surveyed 24 percent said that someone whose income they depended on had been unemployed while they were in college (Undergraduate Survey, 2009). The price of college and the cost of textbooks has escalated. Between the 2009 and 2011 academic years, college tuition and fees rose more than 15 percent at community colleges, 11 percent at public four-year colleges, and 9 percent at four-year privates (College Board, 2011). Loans were harder to obtain and frightening for students to assume. More than seven in ten students (72 percent) who had college loans reported some or major concern about their ability to repay them (Undergraduate Survey, 2009). Student affairs officers told us "financial assistance is just never enough." There are continuing pleas for more financial aid and jobs (Student Affairs Survey, 2011). One institution told us its pool of full-pay applicants had fallen by 70 percent and its full-need group had doubled. In a November–December 2011 survey of college students by the Harvard University Institute of Politics, 70 percent said the economy is the issue that concerns them most (Institute of Politics, 2011)

A small number of student affairs officers said the economic downturn politicized students at their colleges, turning their attention to issues such as sustainability, ensuring a "living wage" for the lowest paid employees on the campus, income inequity, and protesting the governor's proposed budget. Others saw just the opposite impact—isolating students because they were working so many hours and forcing their heads down to focus on their own problems (Student Affair Survey, 2011).

September 11

When the World Trade Center and Pentagon were attacked, the class of 2012 was eleven years old. The United States has been at war half of their lives, since they were in sixth grade. In the minds of many students, September 11, the War on Terror, and the wars in Afghanistan and Iraq are intertwined and very difficult to separate. "9/11 [was] the domino," said one student. Others highlighted the dominoes that fell after September 11 include the wars, the Patriot Act, Abu Ghraib, Guantanamo Bay prison, and rendition (the practice of transporting terrorist suspects to other countries for interrogation or imprisonment). There were deep divisions over immigration, civil liberties, foreign students, discrimination, human rights, and globalization. A student newspaper editor at a northeastern liberal arts college said, "9/11 unified the country . . . the war then tore it apart."

The wars have had a disillusioning effect on undergraduates. More than three out of five held negative opinions of former president Bush (66 percent) and former vice president Dick Cheney (61 percent). Sixty-one percent believed meaningful social change could not be achieved through traditional politics. They wanted the wars over. More than two-thirds thought the US government was wrong to send troops into Afghanistan in the wake of September 11 (68 percent) and 69 percent wanted an immediate withdrawal of US forces from Iraq (Undergraduate Survey, 2009). In fact, the last US troops left Iraq in a staged withdrawal concluding in December 2011.

Contrary to media portrayals, the death of Osama bin Laden did not produce an orgy of giant keg parties and a Mardi Gras atmosphere at America's colleges. Half of the site-visit campuses had little or no visible reaction, which surprised several of the senior student affairs officers. At the other half, there were palpable expressions of relief and happiness. On one campus, the reaction was solemn—students placed flags on the quad for every life lost due to September 11. On several others, the responses were split with impromptu parties and e-mail blasts inviting students to gather and celebrate with libations and counter e-mails, texts, and discussion saying it was wrong to throw a keg party in response to such an incident (Student Affairs Survey, 2011).

In focus-group interviews, students who were in high school in 2001 were far more likely to say, "My generation is defined by 9/11" than those still in elementary school. As one student government president explained, "for younger people [September 11] tends to not come to the forefront as much. They tend to focus more on the impact of having troops in Iraq."

However, all across the country, students, whether they believed September 11 to be a defining moment for their generation or not, told us it was a day they will never forget, frequently comparing it to the assassination of President Kennedy for their parents.

- "I know where I was when I heard about it, which is what you always hear about Kennedy."

- "I remember where I was and what I was wearing and what clip I had in my hair."

- "I just think that our generation is gonna say I know where I was when that happened. . . . like my parents know where they were when the Kennedy assassination [occurred]."

- "You can literally ask anyone on this campus—where were you when you heard the towers had been hit and every one of them will have their story to tell. It's just like JFK for our parent's generation. Everyone can say where they were when JFK was assassinated to this day and it will be very much the same for our generation for 9/11."

Students spoke of the horror of watching the event endlessly on television, seeing the planes hit the World Trade Center and the towers collapse. But there is a difference between having an event seared into a generation's memory and that event having a major impact on their lives.

When we asked about the effect of September 11 on student and campus life, the answers varied dramatically. A frequent response from student affairs officers (29 percent) in an unstructured survey question was little or none. (Student Affairs Survey, 2008). One dean put it this way: there were "immediate effects, but responses have returned to normalcy." A student government president said, "I think a lot of people have forgotten already."

Students who dismissed the importance of September 11 did so for a variety of reasons, some understandable and others troubling. They said it was like Oklahoma City; it happened across the country; it has happened in other countries as well: the United States killed more people; it happens all the time in my neighborhood: people get killed; it happened when I was in fifth grade; it didn't involve anyone I knew; it was overshadowed by more recent and continuing events—Afghanistan, Iraq, and the War on Terror; and echoing the student government president, it was a long time ago.

At the same time, we were also told campuses and students had changed in a number ways in the aftermath of September 11. Without a doubt new courses on September 11, the wars, and Islam were added to the curriculum as well as more international content to existing courses at colleges from coast to coast. There are annual memorials of one sort or another at some of the site-visit colleges, though the number has declined over time.

Undergraduates talked about feeling the world after the attacks was "scary," "sketchy," and "dangerous." Student affairs officers said students had a diminished sense of well-being, became closer to family, and were more fearful and suspicious. When surveyed, 35 percent of the senior student affairs officers said their campus initiated enhanced security measures and safety plans as a consequence (Student Affairs Survey, 2008). This was no doubt reinforced by the student murders at Virginia Tech in 2007. In this area, September 11 may have had more impact on colleges and universities than students. Whether a consequence of the increased security on campus or changing times, a declining percent of students worried about becoming victims of a violent crime—22 percent in 2009 versus 33 percent in 1993 (Undergraduate Survey, 1993, 2009).

The other frequently mentioned consequence of September 11 noted by deans and students was a growing international focus on the part of undergraduates. Students confirmed that interest. More than four out of five students surveyed said they were "very interested in global issues (Undergraduate Survey, 2009). However, their interest was not matched by knowledge of the world. When given a list of current heads of states and asked the degree to which they held positive or negative opinions of them, a majority of students did not know the names of Hu Jintao of China (80 percent), Robert Mugabe of Zimbabwe (72 percent), Nicolas Sarkozy of France (69 percent), Mahmoud Ahmadinejad of Iran (60 percent), and Kim Jong Il of North Korea (60 percent) (Undergraduate Survey, 2009).

This underlines a very important characteristic of current student politics and worldview. They are indeed more interested in international issues than their peers interviewed in the prior studies but their interest is not geopolitical. It is not deep and does not rest on historic institutions. It is more of a sense of being citizens of the world and recognizing that some issues such as population and climate control are global and require concerted international action. Today's students are issue oriented and very "green."

The Election of Barack Obama

The 2008 presidential election brought out 62 percent of college-educated voters aged eighteen to twenty-nine and two-thirds of those young people voted for Barack Obama (CIRCLE, 2008, 2009). Obama appealed to college students for five reasons.

First, Obama's message was change, "change you can believe in." At the time of the election, most college students had lived through three presidencies—Bush, Clinton, and Bush—in a nation deeply divided over religion, economics, social mores, civil liberties, the role and scale of government, and fundamental values. Each of the presidencies was embattled—one over taxes and the economy, a second ostensibly over a sex scandal, the third over war and the economy. For most of their lives, government had been gridlocked. College students wanted change. More than four out of five college students (82 percent) said Americans were not doing enough to bring about changes in our society (Undergraduate Survey, 2009).

Second, Obama focused on the issues students cared about most. Undergraduates said their biggest issues in the 2008 campaign were the economy (42 percent) and the wars (15 percent), No other issue rose to the double digit levels of concern (Undergraduate Survey, 2009).

Third, Obama represented generational change. Ten successive presidents beginning with Franklin Roosevelt and concluding with George H. W. Bush had served during World War II. Bill Clinton and George Bush were early baby boomers. Barack Obama was at the tail end of the boom, born a decade and a half after them.

Fourth, Obama used digital media to communicate with young people. S. Craig Watkins in his book *Young and Digital* described the extent and impact of these efforts (Watkins, 2009). In 2006, Bowdoin student Meredith Segal created a Facebook group, "Students for Barack Obama." Eight months later, there were eight chapters and sixty-two thousand affiliated college students. One member, Farouk Olu Aregbe, created a site, "One Million Strong for Obama." In an hour, there were one hundred members; in five days ten thousand members; in three weeks nearly two hundred thousand members; and on inauguration day, over 940,000 members. In 2007, Senator Obama gave a little-advertised speech at George Mason University, expecting an audience of perhaps one. There were 3,500 in attendance owing largely to Facebook publicity.

Obama hired a young staff to create a new media strategy for his campaign, taking the pioneering efforts of the 2004 Howard Dean presidential campaign of 2004 to a whole new level. They made use of Facebook, Myspace, YouTube, Twitter, LinkedIn, Black Planet, Flickr, and much more. There were Obama games and ads on the hottest, biggest-selling digital games such as *Guitar Hero III, NBA Live 09*, and *NASCAR 09*. The campaign e-mailed, texted, tweeted, and hosted YouTube videos. They texted the choice of vice president, posted on Flickr personal family pictures taken on election night, and e-mailed the Obama agenda after the election. By election night viewers watched more than thirty times as many hours of Obama videos as McCain videos. When the campaign ended, the communication continued.

Fifth, Obama was a black-skinned, multiracial man and the young voters were a diverse generation for whom historic racial divisions were weakening. The overwhelming majority of college students reported having at least one close friend of a different race among Asians (86 percent), whites (80 percent), Hispanics (79 percent), and blacks (70 percent). They were comfortable with interracial dating and marriage (81 percent), more so than the students in the previous survey (64 percent) (Undergraduate Survey, 1993). The comfort extended across races: whites (82 percent), Hispanics (81 percent), blacks (80 percent), and to a lesser extent Asians (68 percent) (Undergraduate Survey, 2009). They were at the vanguard of a nation in which 15 percent of all marriages were interracial in 2008, 9 percent of white marriages, 16 percent of black, 26 percent of Hispanic, and 31 percent of Asian marriages, which is somewhat at odds with the opinions expressed by Asians about intermarriage (Pew Research Center, 2010). The parents of current college students were the generation that broke the religious barriers to intermarriage. Their children may be the group that breaks the racial divides.

Obama received a majority of white (54 percent), Hispanic (76 percent), and black (95 percent) votes from persons aged eighteen to twenty-nine (CIRCLE, 2008).[2] When asked how important a number of factors were in choosing whom to vote for in the 2008 presidential election, policy positions finished first (84 percent) and race was last (11 percent), as shown in Table 1.5 (Undergraduate Survey, 2009).

Table 1.5   Important Factors in Voting for a Presidential
Candidate in 2008 (by Percent)

Proposed policies or strategies	84
Political party	42
Leadership experience	42
Vice-presidential running mate	36
Age	22
Race	11

Source: Undergraduate Survey (2009).

Conclusion

The campuses we visited and the students we encountered
during the course of this study were more like their counterparts
of the 1970s and 1990s than they were different. However, four
events had a powerful impact on current undergraduates, which
was palpable in every aspect of college and student life that we
examined—academics; life beyond the classroom; how students
spend their time and relate to one another and their families,
professors, and others; their political and social attitudes and
activities; and their aspirations and expectations for the future.

The nature, scale, and duration of the impact of each are
likely to vary substantially. The advent of the web and the fact
that this is the first generation of digital natives promises to be
the most fundamental, even disruptive change, with the capacity to transform higher education and the nation in the years to
come. The consequences of the recession are so far short term and
typical of previous economic downturns though far more severe
and wide ranging—bringing about shifts in enrollment patterns,
curriculum choices, financial need, time use, and life expectations. However, the repercussions are as yet uncertain, and not
to be melodramatic, they may be far more profound, affecting

career choices, economic opportunity and attainment, and the future of the American Dream. September 11 and its aftermath can be seen primarily in student political attitudes and interests, their beliefs about government, and their outlook regarding the future. The Obama election is reflected in the state of campus diversity, the call of public service, and perhaps ultimately generational succession.

The chapters that follow describe the current generation of college students—in the classroom, outside the classroom, their relationships with parents, their diversity, and their views regarding the future. The final chapter paints a picture of a future of profound change in which today's students will live their lives, explains why students are ill prepared for that world, and proposes an education needed by students to prepare them to live in that world. It finds that colleges and universities will have to change substantially if they are to provide students with that education. Parents, government, and employers will also need to act.

Notes

1. The character Harry Potter, who was ten years old when the series began, was born three years before the members of the class of 2012 (Rowling, 1997).

2. Data on Asians were unavailable.

2

Academics

THE INTERNET AND THE BLACKBOARD

*People won't necessarily turn their phone off . . . but
put it on vibrate. You can still hear it while the
teacher's lecturing. Then they actually answer
it and they're like, "I am in class."*

—STUDENT

*Text messaging, listening to iPods, you name it,
I've seen it done. I've probably done half of it myself.*

—STUDENT

THIS IS a pragmatic, career-oriented generation. Since
the time of the earliest universities, a millennium ago, the
principal reasons for attending college have been practical: jobs
and money. Learning for learning's sake has never been a prime
motivator.

In this sense, this generation is no different than the ones that
came before it. But their view of the value of higher education and
their goals for college are more utilitarian than their predecessors of

the past four decades, as might be expected for a generation facing a poor job market. Two out of three undergraduates (67 percent) say the chief benefit of a college education is that it increases one's earning power (Undergraduate Survey, 1969, 1976, 1993, 2009).

Current undergraduates want career skills and knowledge from college. Nearly three out of four, a proportion that has risen steadily since the 1969 survey, say obtaining a detailed grasp of a special field (74 percent) and training and skills for an occupation (73 percent) is essential. In fact, students (75 percent) want their colleges to put greater emphasis on these things and many would also like them to provide access to a social network that will help professionally (43 percent). If they could get the same job now or after graduation, 45 percent would take it now, which is a greater number than in past surveys.

By contrast, the percentage of undergraduates who rate as essential nonmaterial goals, such as formulating values and goals for their lives (52 percent) and learning to get along with people (38 percent), has declined significantly since 1969. Students eschew the more frivolous reasons one might go to college—to have fun for a few years before getting a job, to get out of the house, and to find a spouse (see Table 2.1) (Undergraduate Survey, 1969, 1976, 1993, 2009).

Despite the greater vocational orientation among students, their choice of majors has remained relatively constant for the past forty years. Slightly more than three in five students have chosen professional fields of study versus slightly less than two in five have selected the traditional arts and sciences subjects. Within professional studies, however, there have been major shifts Business has become the most popular of all majors, accounting for roughly a fifth of all students throughout the period. Education has been the big loser because other more prestigious jobs traditionally reserved for white males opened to women and people of color in the 1970s. Once the most popular major in the 1960s and early 1970s, education plummeted in concentrators during the

Table 2.1   Student Goals for College (Percent Who Agree)

	1969	1976	1993	2009
The chief benefit of a college education is that it increases one's earning power.		44	57	67
Essential goal for college: to get a detailed grasp of special field	62	68	71	74
Essential goal for college: to get training and skills for an occupation	59	67	70	73
Colleges should place more emphasis on specialized training for a career.				75
Essential goal for college: access to a social network that will help you professionally				43
Essential goal for college: to formulate life values and goals for my life	71	62	52	50
Essential to learn to get along with people at college	76	66	47	38
If I could get a job now or get the same job after college, I would take it now.		38	38	45
Essential goal for college: to have fun for a few years before getting a job				17
Essential goal for college: to get away from home				15
Essential goals for college: to find a spouse				6

Source: Undergraduate Surveys (1969, 1976, 1993, 2009).

1970s and has continued to shed majors since. The principal beneficiary of the decline was business, to which women and minorities migrated from education. Engineering also dropped whereas health; security and protective services; parks, recreation, and leisure studies; and communications grew (see Table 2.2).

Table 2.2 Most Frequent Majors of Bachelor's Degree Recipients: 1970–1971 to 2008–2009 (by Percent)

	1970–1971	1980–1981	1990–1991	2000–2001	2008–2009
Agriculture	2	2	1	2	2
Architecture	1	1	1		1
Area, ethnic, and gender studies					1
Biological sciences	4	5	4	5	5
Business	14	21	23	21	22
Communication and journalism	1	3	5	5	5
Computer and information sciences		2	2	4	2
Education	21	12	10	8	6
Engineering	5	7	6	5	4
English	8	3	5	4	3
Family and consumer sciences	1	1	1	1	1
Foreign language	3	1	1	1	1
Health professions	3	7	5	6	8
Liberal arts, general studies, and humanities	1	2	3	3	3

Math and statistics	3	1	1	1	1
Multidisciplinary studies		1	2	2	2
Parks, recreation, leisure, and fitness		1		1	2
Philosophy and religion	1	1	1	1	1
Physical science	3	3	1	1	1
Psychology	5	4	5	6	6
Public administration and social services		2	1	2	1
Security and protection		1	1	2	3
Social sciences and history	18	11	11	10	11
Visual and performing arts	4	4	4	5	6
Arts and sciences total	50	35	36	37	38

Source: National Center for Education Statistics (2010).

The increasing career orientation of undergraduates has not raised their degree aspirations. Three out of five students are planning to pursue graduate studies, which was also the case in the prior two surveys (Undergraduate Survey, 1976, 1993, 2009).

For this generation, the two-year associate and four-year baccalaureate degree have become a thing of the past. A study of 2008 bachelor degree recipients found that the average time to earn a degree for those who began at community colleges was five and one-quarter years; only a quarter of the students graduated within four years. For students who started at four-year colleges, 44 percent of degree recipients at public universities earned their bachelor degrees in four years and at private institutions the proportion rose to 65 percent (National Center for Institute of Education Sciences, 2011).

The slowdown can be attributed to several factors. More students are working more hours and cannot take full-time course loads; part-time enrollment is increasing owing to an aging student body; and it is becoming increasingly difficult for students to find the courses they need to graduate, overwhelmingly a problem at public universities. Students complained that too few sections of required courses were offered; classes were offered in the wrong sequence such that prerequisites sometimes followed the courses for which they were prerequisite; and not infrequently classes were just not offered when they were scheduled. One student explained that courses at his large public university seemed to be offered when faculty felt like teaching them rather than when students needed them. The recession has also been a contributing factor. One dean of students noted that when faculty members took sabbaticals, their courses more frequently were not taught while they were gone.

Nonetheless, the students are satisfied with college (79 percent), the same percentage as in the 1993 survey, but a higher proportion than ever before (83 percent) say they would rather be going to college than doing anything else. They are interested in most of their courses (80 percent) and think they are relevant to the world outside college (78 percent). This generation does not want major changes in the programs they take. They don't want all courses to be elective (67 percent), faculty tenure to be eliminated (67 percent), or grades to be abolished (81 percent). They are more satisfied with the quality of teaching at their colleges (87 percent) than their predecessors. They think their professors enjoy teaching (77 percent) and believe teaching effectiveness rather than publication should be the primary criterion for promotion (77 percent) (Undergraduate Survey, 1993, 2009).

Current undergraduates have stronger and richer relationships with faculty members than the students previously surveyed. They are more likely to have professors whom they can turn to for advice on personal matters (61 percent), who take a personal interest in their academic progress (76 percent), and who have had an influence on their academic careers (78 percent) (Undergraduate Survey, 1976, 1993, 2009).

This is not to say that student-faculty relations are now a panacea. Small but significant numbers of students report faculty members have made them feel uncomfortable or unwelcome in class (28 percent), made them doubt their abilities (25 percent), and had a strong negative influence on their careers (18 percent) (Undergraduate Survey, 2009). In all cases, positive and negative regarding their experiences with faculty members, the responses were slightly higher at four-year colleges (see Table 2.3).

Grades are one of the more curious aspects of this generation. Grade inflation continues. More than two in five students report grade point averages of A- or higher, the greatest proportion in more than forty years, whereas just 5 percent say they have grades of C or less, the lowest percentage in more than forty years. So it is not wholly surprising that the percentage of students who say grades should be abolished has plummeted over this time period. What is surprising though is that 60 percent of all students believe their

Table 2.3 Academic Experience and Values (Percent Who Agree)

	1969	1976	1993	2009
I plan to earn a graduate degree.		61	61	58
I am satisfied with college overall.	62	71	79	79
I would rather be going to college than doing anything else.	69	69	75	83
I am not interested in most of my courses.		38	20	20
Much of what is taught at my college is irrelevant to what is going on in the outside world.	42	29	28	28
Undergraduate education would be improved if all courses electives.		35	23	33
Undergraduate education would be improved if faculty tenure was eliminated.				33
Undergraduate education would be improved if grades were abolished.	53	32	21	19
I am satisfied with teaching at my college.	67	72	81	87
There are professors I feel free to turn to for advice on personal matters.		53	52	61
There are professors who take an interest in my academic progress.		64	65	73
There are professors who have had a great influence on my academic career.		56	54	75

There are professors who have helped me to recognize my abilities academically or intellectually.	77
There are professors who have made me feel uncomfortable or unwelcome in their class.	28
There are professors who have made me doubt my abilities academically or intellectually.	25
There are professors who had a strong negative influence on my academic career.	18
My professors act like they genuinely enjoy teaching.	89

Source: Undergraduate Survey (1969, 1976, 1993, 2009).

grades understate the true quality of their work and 46 percent of students say they are not doing as well as they would like academically.

These sentiments need to be placed in context. Six out of ten community college and three out of ten four-year college students, numbers that have grown with each survey, are taking remedial or basic skills courses. The proportion of students taking remedial courses has increased with each survey (see Table 2.4). At almost two-thirds (66 percent) of two-year colleges and 29 percent of four-year schools surveyed in 2008, the number of students taking remedial courses had increased since 2001. At only 1 percent of the schools had the percentage declined. It is also true that most college students (54 percent) rate their courses as difficult or very difficult. Less than one in ten (7 percent) describe them as easy or very easy (Student Affairs Survey, 2008; Undergraduate Survey, 1976, 1993, 2009).

So how could students possibly believe their inflated grades understate their abilities? There was a story told in a number of our undergraduate focus groups that gives some insight. It is an anecdote, offered to illustrate the arbitrary character and unfairness of grades, about a student who hardly studied and got a higher grade than the storyteller. There is a tendency among the

Table 2.4   Student Grades and Remediation (by Percent)

	1969	1976	1993	2009
My grade point average is A- or higher.	7	19	26	41
My grade point average is C or less.	25	13	9	5
I work hard at my studies.		86	89	93
Hard work always pays off.		79	79	83
I have taken a basic skills or remedial course.		29	32	45

Source: Undergraduate Survey (1969, 1976, 1993, 2009).

students we interviewed to equate quantity with quality, process with outcome. The amount of work given to an initiative is expected to translate directly into the quality of the outcome. Differential ability was rarely mentioned. This generation works hard at their studies (93 percent), believes that hard work always pays off (83 percent), and nine out ten (89 percent) describe themselves as intellectuals (Undergraduate Survey, 2009).

When we told student affairs staff about what the students had said, they generally greeted the news with smiles and head nods. They were not surprised. They used terms such as *coddled, spoiled, never permitted to fail,* and *protected* to describe current students. One captured the feelings of many, saying this is a generation that was never permitted to skin their knees. They all won awards at everything they ever tried—most-improved player, fourth runner-up, best seven-year-old speller born on March 8. They grew up with an inflated sense of accomplishment and expect to continue to receive awards, at least applause, for everything they do.

The most dramatic change in academics between this book and the last is technology. Students, now predominantly digital natives, want a lot more. Four out of five say undergraduate education would be improved if their classes made greater use of technology (78 percent) and if their professors knew more about how to use it (78 percent). A majority (52 percent) want more blended instruction, combining online and in-person classes. A third (33 percent) go even further, asking for more courses to be completely online (Undergraduate Survey, 2009). Indeed, 80 percent of senior student affairs officers surveyed said their campuses were experiencing increasing demand for enhanced technology by students (Student Affairs Survey, 2008).

=====

Students paint a mixed picture of technology use in their current classes, ranging from "it is being used in all my classes" to "I haven't seen it at all" and everything in between. "A lot of professors are breaking into technology—some of them are just kind of getting in there and stumbling, but they are giving it a try." "I have seen it overused." "A lot of people don't know how to use it and some people choose not to use it." But they agree: "the use of technology is going up every year." The staples in college courses are PowerPoint and clickers. Student reactions vary widely. On PowerPoints they say the following:

- "They all use PowerPoint when they lecture and then they will usually e-mail you the PowerPoint."

- "People don't know how to use PowerPoint the right way . . . A teacher will summarize everything you read the night before and just read it."

- "It lets me listen to lectures rather than getting distracted taking notes."

- "They use it as their whole presentation rather than a visual part of the presentation."

- "I am just tired of PowerPoint presentations."

- "It helps."

- "There are so many awful PowerPoint slides that the professors just do for no reason."

Opinions are equally mixed on clickers. On the positive side, students regularly reported, "I actually learn a lot more with them." The negatives are that clickers are expensive; they are upgraded regularly so students need to buy new ones; different professors require different types of clickers, necessitating multiple purchases; and clickers get abused. On a number of campuses, students told us variants of the same story. In a late afternoon class, the day before the Thanksgiving break, in which clickers were used to take attendance, a student brought thirty-five of them to class in his backpack for his fraternity brothers, who had already ready gone home. The room was more than half empty but the attendance records showed it was nearly full. Less dramatically, students told of trading off with roommates. One would go to class and take the other's clicker.

The message from students is that if a faculty member is going to use technology in the classroom, professors need "to have a good handle on what they are doing." If they're "not good at it, teach what you know so I can get the most out of this class." One student put it this way: "The bottom line is technology is not going to make up for a bad teacher."

The familiar tensions between students and faculty members regarding technology and digital media were presented often and animatedly. From the point of view of faculty members, students were criticized for the poverty of their research skills and their attitudes about research. They were chastised for thinking a *Wikipedia* or Google search is adequate for a paper. They were disparaged for not using the library, for not reading books, for not even thinking about consulting a journal, and for being just plain lazy. When the criticism was presented to students, they tended to smile or sometimes roll their eyes, acknowledging the problem or maybe just the conflict. Often, they shrugged off the criticism or told us faculty members are out of step with the times. "They [professors] are so reliant on research and go to the library instead of going to Google." "I have a few classes where professors have openly encouraged students to go to the library and flip through books . . ." "I still use the journals. [I'm] just not walking the halls [of the library]."

These are the symptoms, the daily clashes, the flashpoints, marking the fundamental differences between faculty members and students discussed in Chapter One. Digital natives are being taught by digital immigrants in analog universities. Faculty chafed at student expectations that they would be sitting at their computers twenty-four hours a day waiting to respond to their inquiries "because, you know, Amazon does that." There is no denying that students' attitudes in this matter are annoying, actually infuriating, but more troubling are rising rates of academic dishonesty, plagiarism, and classroom disruption on campus.

Senior student affairs officers report that the number of cheating or plagiarism incidents are up at 57 percent of their campuses, more at four-year colleges (59 percent) than two-year schools (54 percent), and that student understanding of plagiarism has declined to 46 percent of baccalaureate institutions and 25 percent of community colleges (Student Affairs Survey, 2008). We were often told of blatant incidents of plagiarism—a student turning in a paper with "*Time*, September 1990" at the bottom of one of the pages. Part of the problem according to students is that the Internet makes so much high-quality content available, it's too tempting not to use it, and the volume is so vast that it's hard to believe you will get caught.

Cheating is certainly not new in higher education. There is a long history of fraternities and sororities maintaining paper banks, one of the earliest forms of recycling whereby the works of current Greeks could be shared with future generations. For the nonaffiliated, there have been for-profit paper-writing companies, enterprising classmates, and gazillion of other ways to try to beat the system. Digital technology has expanded the possibilities—photographing tests, texting answers, and sneaking electronic cheat sheets into exams. What is different today is that the content is free and only a click away. A dean sympathized, saying "I can understand the seductive power; you know the night before something's due. [They] haven't started doing it for whatever reason—work, kids, whatever. [They] know all the answers in the universe are there and . . . a few clicks away. They succumb . . . often they try to hide it and sometimes they just download it."

The real conundrum, according to senior student affairs officers, is that a growing number of students don't understand why plagiarism is wrong. One nonplussed dean told us he was seeing something he had never seen before. A student comes to his office, caught red-handed turning in a plagiarized paper, and has "no clue" what the problem is. After all, students commonly collaborate with friends online and share with them the content they find on the Internet. So why is it wrong at college?

Not only is there a problem regarding the use of content from the net, there's the issue of where and when students can appropriately use their hardware. Senior student affairs officers on a majority of campuses surveyed (53 percent) reported increases in inappropriate or disruptive classroom behaviors since 2001 (Student Affairs Survey, 2008). As already noted, between 2008 and 2011, nearly half of the campuses surveyed reported rises in technology-based infractions and misbehaviors as well (Student Affairs Survey, 2011). It's the phenomena of texting, vibrating and ringing cell phones, instant messaging, and more in the classroom. Students describe what's going on in the classroom this way:

- "They are ordering things online. They are sending e-mail back and forth. They are playing games in the classroom, doing everything but what they are supposed to be doing."

- "Text messaging, listening to iPods, you name it, I've seen it done. I've probably done half of it myself."

- "You are typing your notes and all of a sudden you kind of wander off to check your e-mail and hey, look at that, someone sent you a message so you go click on Facebook and go to your message and get way distracted."

- "People won't necessarily turn their phone off . . . but put it on vibrate. You can still hear it while the teacher's lecturing. Then they actually answer it and they're like, 'I am in class.'"

- "I keep my phone in my pocket and text without looking."

- "My favorite one was someone actually [having] a DVD and watching a movie."

The result is that faculty members' comfort with students and their behavior has decreased on nearly half of all campuses surveyed (49 percent) and faculty member complaints on these topics has increased at majority of colleges and universities (54 percent) since 2001 (Student Affairs Survey, 2008). Faculty members in some cases have resorted to shutting off WiFi in their classrooms, telling students they will be thrown out of class if their phones ring or vibrate, answering their student phones when they ring ("It's your mother. You better take this."), assigning essays to students whose phones ring or vibrate, and barring visible digital technology in their classrooms.

What to do about inappropriate digital classroom behavior is increasingly part of new faculty-orientation programs. There is much more explanation by professors to their students about what constitutes acceptable classroom behavior and what does not. More and more often, admonitions and codes of conduct are making their way onto syllabi. One dean told us that what we've accepted as normal common sense we now have to spell out for students regarding "what we expect in terms of their behavior in the classroom." But in the spirit of "trust but verify," plagiarism-detecting software is becoming a staple on college campuses.

Another senior student affairs officer said today's college students "are rule followers. They respect authority now. It comes with a twist. They have to be told the rules." He said "syllabi are going to be small volumes soon," including things like "you can't come to class inebriated."

This situation is a conundrum. It is on one hand impossible to believe that students do not understand that using digital devices in a classroom is rude, which certainly seems a product of a coddled generation. On the other hand, it is clear that today's undergraduates, who have grown up in a world dramatically different from their parents, truly do not know the rules by which adults are expected to live their lives and by which their colleges work.

3

Life Outside the Classroom

THE NEW TRIBALISM

I had this guy leave me a voice-mail at work, so I called him at home and then he e-mailed me to my BlackBerry, and so I texted to his cell, and now you just have to go around checking all these different portals just to get rejected by seven different technologies. It's exhausting.

—MARY IN THE MOVIE *HE'S JUST NOT THAT INTO YOU*

THERE IS an irony. Student social life is invading the classroom but it is retreating from the campus. Technology is the vehicle for bringing social life into the classroom and it is the means of replacing social life at the college. The last study found that student social life often occurred in packs, groups of undergraduates, men and women, rather than in couples, and it still does. But social media also allows each student to enlarge the pack to what amounts to a virtual tribe, consisting of friends, family, neighbors, acquaintances, and any other significant people in an undergraduate's life, past or present, and stay connected with that tribe twenty-four hours a day, seven days a week, in class and out. Students live in world of competition between intimacy and isolation. This chapter looks at student life outside the classroom—on campus, face to face, and online.

Campus Life

The campus is becoming an increasingly small part of student social lives. The proportion of undergraduates living in college housing has dropped continually since the first student survey in 1969 (34 percent) to the present (28 percent) (Undergraduate Survey, 1969, 1976, 1993, 2009). Fewer than a third of all students attend on-campus social or community events (33 percent); use the college gym or fitness center (33 percent); attend collegiate athletic events (25 percent); attend meetings of academic or professional clubs (21 percent); attend meetings of student-sponsored clubs (20 percent); or attend lectures, debates, or other academic events (19 percent) once a month or more. More than a third and in most cases many more than a third do none of these things (Undergraduate Survey, 2009). Use of the library is the only exception (see Table 3.1).

Campus life today is largely the province of four-year colleges, where more than half of all college students (58 percent) are residential and others live in off-campus housing. A majority of students attending college part-time or working twenty-one hours a week or more are not involved in campus activities or events either, with the exception of using the library. Undergraduates over the age of twenty-four are also poor attendees of campus events (Undergraduate Survey, 2009) (see Table 3.2).

The bottom line is that campus life is the domain of traditionally aged, full-time students attending four-year colleges and working half-time or less. But even for this group, most of the events a majority attend are not college sponsored. The exceptions are the undergraduates who have the fewest noncollege demands, that is, students who work ten hours a week or less (see Table 3.3).

Table 3.1 Student Attendance of On-Campus Events by Institutional Type (by Percent)

	Two-year colleges		Four-year colleges		Total	
	Once a month or more	Never	Once a month or more	Never	Once a month or more	Never
Attend on campus social or community events	13	57	47	20	33	35
Use the gym or fitness center	7	76	50	36	33	53
Attend lectures, debates, or other academic events	5	69	29	31	19	47
Attend meetings of student-sponsored social clubs	13	78	39	42	20	57
Attend a college athletic event	6	70	38	35	25	49
Attend meetings of academic or professional clubs	8	80	29	50	21	62
Go to the library to study or work on academic assignments	63	22	66	17	63	19

Source: Undergraduate Survey (2009).

Table 3.2 Percent of Students Who Do Not Participate in College Events by Attendance, Hours Worked, and Age (by Percent)

	Attend part-time	Work more than twenty hours a week		Twenty-four years of age or older
		Twenty-one to thirty-five hours	Thirty-six or more	
Attend on campus social or community events	58	52	54	36
Use the gym or fitness center	74	62	71	53
Attend lectures, debates, or other academic events	71	57	65	46
Attend meetings of student-sponsored social clubs	82	66	78	57
Attend a college athletic event	68	56	66	49
Attend meetings of academic or professional clubs	81	78	71	61
Go to the library to study or work on academic assignments	27	16	32	19

Source: Undergraduate Survey (2009).

Table 3.3   Students Who Say Most of the Events and Activities They Attend Are College Sponsored by Selected Student Characteristics (by Percent)

Attend two-year college	13
Attend four-year college	44
All students	31
Attend part-time	14
Attend full-time	36
Work ten hours or less per week	53
Work eleven to twenty hours per week	29
Work twenty-one to thirty-five hours per week	18
Work more than thirty-five hours per week	20
Aged eighteen to twenty-four	33
Aged twenty-five or older	17

Source: Undergraduate Survey (2009).

The economy, which is causing more students to work longer hours, attend college part-time, and extend undergraduate education beyond age twenty-four, is a major cause of low participation rates. Many deans told us that growing numbers of students have the choice of working to put food on the table and pay tuition or attending campus events. But the economy is not the sole cause of the diminished involvement of undergraduates in extracurricular or co-curricular activities. The decline has increased but that was so in the previous study as well.

Face to Face: What Students Do for Fun

When we asked students what they do for fun, the answer's been the same in all three studies: drinking and partying. Further down the list come sports, outdoor recreation, sex, computer games, and sleep, among other activities. What has changed is how they go about doing these things.

Alcohol and Drugs

As in the last study, student drinking most frequently occurs off campus in bars and student lodgings, though Greek houses are also common venues. Students and senior student affairs officers agree that on a majority of four-year campus party nights are Thursday, commonly called Thirsty Thursday (56 percent of four-year schools and 35percent of two-year colleges), Friday (85 percent of four-year schools and 46 percent of two-year colleges), and Saturday (88 percent of four-year colleges and 75 percent of two-year schools) (Student Affairs Survey, 2008).

Everyone on campus can drink legally or illegally; colleges are awash in alcohol and fake IDs. The problem is not so much underage drinking as it is how much students drink. Deans of students describe binge drinking and alcohol abuse as the prime mental health issue on campus. Here's how several described the situation:

- "What dominates our social scene is alcohol and alcohol abuse, kids drinking to get shit-faced and even sort of more as a social lubricant—at levels that I don't quite understand. It confounds us. We drank, but we didn't want to black out or get sick. There is the glorification of alcohol and partying. They do weird things. We have real party issues here because of the nature of the community. It's . . . just young people without the social governors that a mixed population provides."

- "It's not a new issue, it goes back many generations. [What's changed is that] they turn away from beer and [are] into drinking hard alcohol and the flavored vodkas particularly are new. So there is a lot of pre-partying and slamming alcohol before you get to an event and I think we are seeing more issues with how women drink. So we've been struggling with alcohol poisoning."

- "Binge drinking used to be the old standard five drinks on one occasion. We now see students who will do twelve or more on one occasion and that is very alarming."

- "Because there is a risk with drinking socially [because they are underage] there is a lot of binge drinking going on pre-party, before they go out. And then what happens if they to go out and drinks are available, their judgment is totally shot because they have just downed eight or ten shots. And then they end up in a situation where people are having fifteen drinks and blood alcohol levels of .25 and up."

- "It is a freshman-sophomore phenomenon. Then they mature and say I don't want to be that stupid anymore."

Nearly a quarter of colleges and universities (24 percent), more at four-year colleges (31 percent) than community colleges (14 percent) report rises in binge drinking since 2001. Between 2008 and 2011, a quarter (23 percent) also experienced increases in alcohol consumption (Student Affairs Survey, 2008, 2011). A majority of college students at four-year colleges (51 percent) think alcohol abuse is a serious problem on their campuses. At community colleges, only one-fifth of the students (21 percent) surveyed agree (Undergraduate Survey, 2009).

Among college seniors, one in three (33 percent) say they missed a class because of alcohol or drug use. More than a quarter report they drank alcohol heavily with the goal of passing out (29 percent) and got lower grades on a course or assignment because of alcohol or drug use (27 percent). More than one in five (23 percent) engaged in unplanned or unprotected sex because of alcohol or drug use (Undergraduate Survey, 2009). And senior student affairs officers indicate that the date rape cases they deal with overwhelmingly involve alcohol.

As to why students drink so much, there are lots of different explanations. There's stress relief. A southern research university student affairs vice president told us, "They have high stress lives. These students work hard. They do extracurriculars. They study a lot. They take heavy course loads. They will double, triple major. They will do community services. And . . . they self-medicate with alcohol in order to break out of that multitasking, to be able to kick back and relax."

A student echoed the sentiments of many of his generation, saying he drank because he had lived at home until he went to college and he was free at college to do what he wanted, to experiment, to have a good time. Over and over students said, "it's fun." With delight, they told us about the drinking games they played.

Drinking was also a way to reduce social and sexual inhibitions, which may in part reflect time spent alone in front of computer monitors. This didn't seem to us a very good explanation for binge drinking and throwing up or passing out.

Still another rationale was peer pressure. Students repeatedly said, "I have a lot of friends who think they can't have any fun unless they have a few drinks." "It severely curtails my social life because I am an alcoholic and can't drink. I spend a lot of Saturday nights alone in my room." Another nondrinker explained, "I get a lot of grief from a lot of people who are drinking and people try to make me drink. . . . There is definitely a lot of peer pressure . . . A very, very good friend of mine whom I've known since my freshman year came in with the same mind-set as me and then half way through our sophomore year kind of decided, oh, I can't resist the peer pressure anymore and then went and got drunk every single night and turned into this crazy partier . . . Peer pressure is tough." The peer pressure and belief that drinking was the only way to have a good time was more vehemently and frequently expressed in this study than its predecessors.

We also talked with students about drug use. When we asked them what the drug of choice was on their campuses, the most common response was that alcohol is number one "far and away. Pot is second, but it's not nearly as close." There were, of course, exceptions. At one isolated liberal arts college undergraduates said it was easier for underage students to get marijuana than alcohol. We were also told on several sectarian campuses that drinking and marijuana were harshly dealt with, so student use was relatively low, well hidden, and generally occurred off campus. Yet another answer was tobacco. Hookah bars seemed to be springing up near many of the campuses we visited and were popular with students.

Reports by college seniors confirm the conventional wisdom. Alcohol is, in fact, their drug of choice. Marijuana and tobacco follow second. Hallucinogens and unprescribed sedatives are a very distant third. All other unprescribed or illegal drugs have been tried by less than one in ten students (see Table 3.4).

Marijuana use is up since 2001, more at four-year colleges where 43 percent of institutions surveyed reported increases than community colleges (19 percent). This was not a serious concern for student affairs staff. There is a fairly bright line in the minds of undergraduates we interviewed between marijuana, which is viewed as a common recreational drug, and hard drugs such as heroin and cocaine, though there was the recognition that marijuana is a gateway to the harder substances. On a number of campuses, we were told of large, public, and spirited 420 celebrations, April 20, which is the international day for people to gather and imbibe cannabis. During this time period, colleges and universities also reported very slight increases in the use of date rape drugs and declines in the consumption of hallucinogens and tobacco (Student Affairs Survey, 2008).

Table 3.4 Drugs College Seniors Report Having Tried at Least Once (by Percent)

Alcohol (currently use)	91
Tobacco or other forms of nicotine	41
Marijuana	41
Stimulant medication not prescribed to me (e.g., Adderall, Ritalin, Provigil)	14
Hallucinogens (e.g., LSD, mescaline, Ecstasy, mushrooms)	12
Sedatives or relaxants not prescribed to me (e.g., barbiturates, Valium, Xanax)	10
Stimulants (e.g., cocaine, crack, amphetamines)	8
Opiates (e.g., opium, heroin, morphine, codeine)	7
Antidepressants not prescribed to me (e.g., Paxil, Prozac, Zoloft, Lexapro)	5
Inhalants (e.g., poppers, nitrous oxide, glue, solvents)	4
Methamphetamines	3
Dissociative drugs (e.g., GHB, Rohypnol [roofies], Ketamine [Special K])	3

Source: Undergraduate Survey (2009).

Senior student affairs officers told us the biggest drug problem at their schools was prescription drug abuse. At the four-year colleges surveyed, more than three out of five (62 percent) said prescription drug abuse had increased. Only 15 percent of community colleges had the same experience, which can in part be chalked up to their commuter populations for whom social life routinely occurs outside of college. However, 20 percent of two-year colleges, often rural, indicated that chemical abuse, usually amphetamines, had increased. Students told us of "people using other people's medicine . . . things like Ritalin . . . for studying." "There's a lot of sharing." Students sell their pain medications for profit because they want money for going out. *Pharming* was a term heard for the first time in this study. It is the practice of mixing drugs or mixing drugs with alcohol or pooling student medications and taking a combination. On one campus, students described a party in which attendees put their meds in a bowl and people reached in and took a handful, sort of like a bowl of M&Ms (Undergraduate Survey, 2009).

The rise in prescription drug abuse can be traced to the fact that there are a lot more drugs on campus. A growing numbers of students are coming to college taking medication. We heard this at colleges from coast to coast—public, private, sectarian, nonsectarian, large, and small. Typical was a western research university where a quarter of the students who come to the campus health center are already on medication. At a southern liberal arts college, 30 percent of their students were using medications. At a northeastern university, the senior student affairs officer said "a fair number of our students are medicated and come to us on antidepressants."

Sex and Romance

There seems to be a lot more sex on campus than romance, which was true in the last study as well. Students continue to hang out in packs, groups of men and women who do things together. "Group activities . . . kind of lead to individual activities and it goes from there," a student explained. When members of groups pair off, it's often through *hook-ups*, which is a rather vague term that can mean kissing, "making out," or having sex. This is not a particularly helpful definition either because *making out* has the same range of meanings as *hooking up* and although having sex definitely refers to vaginal intercourse, it may or may not also include oral-genital and anal intercourse. President Clinton's narrower definition had a goodly number of adherents on college and university campuses. A quarter of all undergraduates (24 percent) believe that being sexually abstinent does not rule out oral or anal sex. The proportion is actually slightly higher for students who classify themselves as religious fundamentalist (31 percent), many of whom are preserving their virginity for marriage (Undergraduate Survey, 2009).

The best counsel on understanding what people mean when they say they *hooked up* came from a student in a focus group at a university with a conservative religious tradition. "It is defined as an intentionally vague term that can mean anything from kissing to casual sex and it varies depending upon how far the individual has gone before. So if you have someone who is sexually active, they will probably use the term *hook up* to mean sex or some form of it. And then 'I made out with her' if they had something less versus a person who is abstaining. If they made out with someone, that would be their definition of a *hook-up*."

Students for the most part described a culture of casual relationships and casual sex. This was less the case at religious colleges, schools with older populations, and institutions serving larger numbers of Hispanic students who were more circumspect in discussing this subject. In truth colleges are diverse places with mixed groups and practices—abstinence groups, committed couples, students who are involved in relationships, students who are not, and all the permutations in between.

But these generalizations can be offered. First, most students are sexually active. As freshmen, a majority of undergraduates have engaged in oral (56 percent) or vaginal sex (61 percent) and a small minority in anal sex (15 percent). As would be expected, the proportions rise over the college years (Undergraduate Survey, 2009).

Second, not all students are hooking up but large numbers are. By the time they graduate from college, about half of all undergraduates (47 percent) have hooked up or had casual sex with someone (Undergraduate Survey, 2009).

Third, only a minority of sexually active college students report more than one partner. In the past twelve months, seven out of ten students report a single partner versus less than two out of ten (17 percent) who have had three or more partners (Undergraduate Survey, 2009).

Fourth, students are more open and explicit about sex than they were in the past studies. A vice president for student life at a western research university made this point when he described the content of a sex advice column that appeared in the student newspaper every Wednesday. "I didn't even know you could do some of the stuff they do. To say it's explicit is an understatement. Just detailed descriptions of vaginas and penises and positions and tactics. I'm not a prude," he went on, "so young people screw. That's what they have always done and always will do. We did. But it is different now and the explicit[ness] of it is—I don't know. . . . We're sixties baby boomers, but whoa we can't do that."

Fifth, formal dating seems to be largely a thing of the past. A student patiently explained to us, "I don't think people go on dates per se as much . . . You don't see the traditional guy takes the girl out to dinner and a movie. You don't see that very much." Less than half of freshmen (48 percent) report they have been on a date. Curiously, nearly all seniors say they have (85 percent). When asked to explain the discrepancy, the answer given is that dating has become a plan by a couple to do something together. "It's not a date date" like in the day.

Sixth, students say they know what safe sex is, but many don't practice it. Among unmarried students, a quarter say they think they know what constitutes safe sex and three-quarters say they are very well informed. Yet 39 percent say they never, rarely, or only sometimes use a condom during vaginal intercourse, 62 percent report this in regard to anal intercourse, and 89 percent indicate this is the case with regard to oral sex (Undergraduate Survey, 2009). This is true even though many of the campuses we visited made condoms very easily and anonymously available.

Iowa State University has happy hump day, condom days on Wednesday, when condoms are being given out on the steps of the library. At University of Wisconsin, Milwaukee, there is a formal program of condom bingo played in the cafeteria in which the markers are the condoms. At Swarthmore there are free condoms at the health center and the director reports thousands are picked up each year. At Lewis and Clark, they are given away at the women's center. Resident assistants leave them in baggies on their doors, refilling them often, at several universities.

Seventh, dating has become more diverse. Interracial dating is up at 22 percent at two-year colleges and 37 percent of four-year schools. Gay, lesbian, bisexual, and transgender dating has increased at 17 percent of community colleges and 41 percent of baccalaureate-granting institutions (Student Affairs Survey, 2008).

Eighth, sexual harassment and stalking has also increased slightly on college campuses, much more at four-year schools than two-year colleges (see Table 3.5).

But what stood out in student descriptions of sex and relationships was the lack of romance associated with it. A small minority said there continued to be romance at college—"you can be extremely romantic on this campus"—and told of picnics, special occasions, and senior couples who met freshman year and

Table 3.5 Increases in Sexual Assault, Harassment, and Stalking by Institutional Type (by Percent)

	Two-year school	Four-year school	Total
Sexual assault	5	6	6
Physical stalking or harassment	6	6	6
Cell phone stalking or harassment	15	41	30
Internet or e-mail stalking or harassment	15	55	39

Source: Student Affairs Survey (2008).

still held hands as they walked together on campus. A female upper-class student said there was still "romance, but no chivalry." Students told us of seriously committed couples, often ascribing that status to upper classmen.

But the absence of romance was plainly apparent when we asked students to tell us the terminology that was used to describe sexual relationships. Neither of us remembers anyone mentioning *making love*, which may be a dated expression today, though small numbers used words like *intimate relations* and *committed relationships*. What we heard far more often were decidedly unromantic terms: *ball, bang, bed buddies, blow job*, and many variants thereof such as *booty call, coitus, do, fuck, hook up, intercourse, one-night stand, poke, score, screw, sex*, and *shag*. There were also specialized terms such as *friends with benefits*, which refers to casual sex between couples who are essentially friends. *Fall back* is the person with whom one has a recurring sexual relationship and is called when there are no better prospects. *Hallcest* and *dormcest* mean having sex with someone who lives on your floor or in your dormitory. *LUG* is an acronym for lesbian until graduation. *Sexiled* is when a student has to sleep in another room because his or her roommate is entertaining. A focus group student told us *the walk of shame*, when a woman walks embarrassedly back to the dorm the morning after in the same clothes she wore the night before, is now also called the *stride of pride*.

In talking about sex, there was also often an absence of affection and intimacy. It is "pleasure oriented as opposed to relationship or commitment." "It's kind of like they don't even care about the emotional aspect of it." "It's just sex. Who cares?" "If it feels good, do it." "I like you, let's have sex, and be sex buddies, but not have a real relationship." It's "just exchanging body fluids."

Students often seemed more interested in encounters than continuing relationships, frequently labeling continuing relationships as continuing encounters. A student at a midwestern university described the situation. "One of my friends was like, 'oh yeah, we're dating,' and I said, 'oh, you are boyfriend/girl friend?' She said, 'he's not my boyfriend, we're just dating.'"

Nowhere is this reluctance to move from encounters to relationships more apparent than in the process by which people transition from hook-ups to more permanent status. Over and over, it was described this way:

> You might meet someone at a party and hook up and then if you like them that night, then you might check them out on Facebook. Then you might agree to show up together [independently in the sense that you both might be there] at the same party and that might also end up with hooking up or not hooking up. Then after a succession or a certain number of meetings like that you might decide to start dating each other. Then at some point you will note it on your Facebook that [you are in a relationship].

On some campuses, women with committed relationships that began on Facebook are called *Facebook brides*, a take-off on *mail-order brides*. This makes sense in a culture in which a mark of intimacy is sharing Facebook passwords.

The reason for this behavior did not appear to be a strong desire to remain free and avoid commitments in that 89 percent of undergraduates say having a good marriage or committed relationship is an essential life goal. Rather it seemed more a fear of rejection from a generation that had avoided skinning their knees. It is a risk to express feelings. There is a chance of getting hurt. Dancing alone together is safer.

Virtual Life: The New Tribalism

What is fundamentally different about social life for current undergraduates is that via social media most have created their own communities, small towns or tribes of family, friends, and people with shared interests and experiences on and off campus. Sites such as Facebook, Myspace, and LinkedIn make it possible to find, connect, and communicate with friends, twenty-four hours a day, seven days a week. They enable students to link their lives with the members of their tribe, to share their latest personal information, post a newsfeed giving moment-by-moment status updates, pictures, videos, a wall for messages, e-mail, texting, chatting, gaming, interest groups, event planning and notification, and apps galore. They provide a vehicle for new students to meet their classmates before they ever arrive on campus, to bring college communities together to celebrate and to grieve, to post events, to campaign for student government, to announce protests, parties, and presentations. Perhaps that's why a number of students referred to it as *electronic crack*.

The various social networking sites have attracted very different populations. Facebook has a more educated, white, and affluent population. The members of Myspace are more likely to be people of color, high school students, and lower income individuals. LinkedIn users are older and more professional. A Pew Research Center study found that 92 percent of social network users were on Facebook, 29 percent used Myspace, 18 percent were on LinkedIn, and 13 percent used Twitter (Pew Internet and American Life Project, 2011).

Facebook is the site of choice in America's colleges and universities. A majority of four-year college students (59 percent) check their social networking sites at least once a day, though usage is considerably lower at community colleges (38 percent) (Undergraduate Survey, 2009). A 2011 Pew Research Center study of American adults using social network sites found that on an average day, 15 percent of Facebook users update their status, 22 percent comment on another's posts or status, 20 percent comment on another user's photos, 26 percent "like" another's content, and 10 percent send another user a private message (Pew Internet and American Life Project, 2011).

The college students we surveyed reported having an average of 241 Facebook "friends" (Undergraduate Survey, 2009). Our initial reaction was who has 241 friends? But as of this writing, Diane has 323 friends and Arthur has 237.

We hypothesized that students using social networking sites were competitive regarding the number of friends they had. That is, they prized quantity over quality. There was very little evidence that this was the case. Only one in seven students (14 percent) surveyed agreed with the statement that the more friends I have on Facebook the better I feel and just slightly more (18 percent) worried they did not have enough friends. Only half said they had more friends on Facebook than they did in their everyday life, which seemed to us that Facebook provided a rather expansive definition of friendship (Undergraduate Survey; 2009).

In fact, social networking users appear to have been discriminating in "friending" people. Among adults, the Pew study found their friends consist of people from high school (22 percent), extended family (12 percent), coworkers (10 percent), college friends (9 percent), immediate family (8 percent), people from voluntary groups (7 percent), and neighbors (2 percent) (Pew Internet and American Life Project, 2011). Among college students, the percentages most certainly differ but the constitution of their tribe is likely similar. Undergraduates specifically mentioned teachers, little league, Girl Scout, church, camp, and grade school friends.

The college students surveyed reported that they spoke with or saw a third of their social networking friends during the past six months (Undergraduate Survey, 2009). They use social media to supplement their face-to-face relationships rather than substitute for them. A dean said it this way: "These devices have been used as tools to facilitate student interaction, not replace it." Students gave much evidence that this was the case:

- "There still the traditional meeting in the class, meeting in the club, meeting someone . . . downtown . . . so Facebook is just another step in building relationships."

- "I have a lot of friends from high school or a lot of friends [who went] to other colleges or friends who have transferred to other colleges or people who graduated from here I am trying to keep track of, so it is a really nice to keep in touch with everyone and have access to people."

- "It is kind of a snapshot of what's going on in my friends' lives that I am not immediately around. So I can check my high school friends. You see pictures of what they are doing and have done. You get to see their interests updated and kind of how that has changed and [is] shifting."

- "I'm from Canada so I've got a lot of friends back there and I keep in touch with them through Facebook."

- "My best friend . . . is in Iraq."

- "I use it to communicate with my intramural teams to remind them of games and we have our schedules posted on there and also I use it for groups for school—like group projects and stuff."

- "I disappeared for two years after high school . . . I got on Facebook [to find my old friends] and some friends from middle school contacted me."

- "All of my really good friends go to colleges extremely far away from me and it is very hard—because I am so busy— to keep up through phone so I drop a Facebook message and keep in contact that way. If they call me I am going to want to have an hour-long conversation and I just can't do that."

In many respects, for undergraduates social networking functions the way the telephone did for their parents. For close friends, who students see every day, Facebook is a way to continue their interaction. It is much like their parents as youngsters calling up friends as soon as they left one another's company and talking all evening long. For friends further away, it takes the place of the long distance phone call, but it does this at larger scale than the one-on-one phone call and requires far less time. In this way, social networking enables students to build a tribe and to keep it informed and involved. In the past, students commonly lost high school friends when they went to college and lost college friends when they got jobs. This doesn't need to happen today and to a great extent it doesn't.

Social networking and the proliferation of digital devices have costs as well as benefits. They do isolate. One senior student affairs officer captured the feelings of many of his peers when she said, "students are more connected with others as in their known associates, but less connected than ever to those immediately around them. It is very common to see multiple people in a common area all talking on cell phones or with ear buds in, but completely oblivious to the people immediately next to them." Student after student told us of whipping out their cell phones as soon as they left class and walking across campus chatting, sometimes in groups with each person on their own phone. They are alone together once again.

The isolation is not only a matter of individuals separate from the rest of the community though that exists to a far greater degree than desirable. Indeed, half of the community college students (51 percent) and a third of the four-year college students (34 percent) surveyed said, "I pretty much keep to myself socially." Over a third (35 percent) said they would be more likely to join a group on Facebook than to join a similar on-campus group (Undergraduate Survey, 2009).

If nothing else, the Internet can also be an extraordinary distraction and time sponge. If people were paid minimum wage for all the time they spent playing the game "Angry Birds," we would be well on our way to paying off the national debt. But for some people the problem is more serious. Between 2001 and 2009, 25 percent of community colleges and 45 percent of four-year institutions reported increases in Internet addiction disorders (Student Affairs Survey, 2008).

The isolation occurs far more often in the form of small groups or tribes separate from the rest of the campus community. For example, the students on their cell phones may have been isolated from the people they were walking with but they were in communication with others, perhaps their social networking tribe. The iPod may have changed music from a group to a more individual experience but the music being listened to by the individual is likely to be or become the product of file sharing or a recommendation to or from a friend with notifications to others via social networking sites. Some students may be spending large numbers of hours in their rooms playing games, but those games may involve many other people online or friends in the room playing with them. The isolation may come in the form of more cultivated relationships within student tribes, consisting of people inside and outside the college, and attenuation of ties to the larger campus community. One student affairs vice president said, "These communication tools should be enlarging students' world and worldviews, but they seem to be doing the opposite by teasing out the circle of friends." Another lamented that in the past, "students would hang out together between classes, get to know each other. . . . Now, however, students immediately whip out their phones after class to converse with someone they already know and pass on the opportunity to get to know someone new." This has not diminished the feeling of being a member of a college community. The proportion of students who said, "I have a sense of community at this institution," jumped from 62 percent in 1993 to 78 percent in the current survey (Undergraduate Survey, 1993, 2009).

A consistent complaint from student affairs staff is that current undergraduates do less well at face-to-face than electronic communication. They told us "students appear to be in greater communication with others, but not in a face-to-face environment." On nearly every campus with residential housing, we were told about roommates having an argument facing back-to-back in the same room, not speaking but furiously texting. Deans told of undergraduates coming to their offices to ask them to fix a roommate problem. When the dean asked what the student had done about the problem so far, the answer was often nothing. He or she had not spoken to the roommate about it and expected the dean to take care of it. A number of students said they preferred to text rather than call people because they felt less vulnerable that way. This was particularly the case with matters of the heart. They feared rejection and texts were less personal. This creates an environment in which things that would best be done in person are relegated to texts and e-mails. Students told of getting break-up texts and messages such as "I don't want to be friends anymore." Almost universally, deans said the current generation of college students had weaker social skills. One went so far as to call them *socially retarded*. Requests for single dormitory rooms are up at three out of five four-year colleges surveyed (Student Affairs Survey, 2008).

An interesting and unrelated phenomenon is that different means of communication are used for different audiences. Texts are for friends and e-mails are for other adults. E-mail has become the equivalent of what letter writing was to their parents and the students use texting in the same way their parents now use e-mail. Such is the difference between immigrants and natives. The immigrants are a generation behind in communications technology.

One consequence of digital communication has been a growing expectation of immediacy—instant information, immediate contact, and split-second responses. Today's college students are an impatient lot. Senior student affairs officers told of receiving e-mails from students saying they would be available for the next twenty minutes to receive a response. Twenty-one minutes later the deans said they could count on a miffed phone call. One dean characterized current college students as the "I want it now generation."

Diphobe, the fear of being without a digital device, seems a reality for most students, and there is a growing belief that time is being wasted if there is a digital device nearby and it isn't being used. Time for contemplation has all but disappeared. This combined with the immediacy of the medium and the poverty of student social skills fans a climate for "flaming," sending scorching, injudicious, and inappropriate messages. Print exchanges don't offer as many clues about meaning as speech and face-to-face interactions do. They are more open to interpretation, so anger and nasty exchanges can quickly spiral out of control. There is "more venting" and "less filtering." As one student affairs vice president put it, "They're not prone to think before they hit the send button and . . . they do some dumb and really uncivil things, feeling somehow that they can just write almost anything . . . I've seen some really awful ones to parking people . . . name calling and stuff. I mean they are obviously angry . . . but they didn't have that kind of internal control to say I'm not going to send this." Remember between 2008 and 2011, 44 percent of colleges and universities surveyed reported increases in technology-related incivility (Student Affairs Survey, 2011).

The boundaries between what is permissible and what is not, between what is public and what is private, have blurred. The result is that stalking is on the rise. On several campuses, Facebook was referred to as Stalker Book. One in six college students surveyed said they had been approached by someone whom they did not know, who said they met on Facebook (Undergraduate Survey, 2009).

The problem is that there is no bright line as to what constitutes active pursuit of a person, what constitutes aggressive pursuit of a person, and what constitutes excessive pursuit of a person. A student said it is very easy to cross the line. "My friends and I use Facebook to check up on people—to look at their pictures, read their newsfeed, see their status change, find out what's going on in their lives. Sometimes they are people we know well. Sometimes they are people we don't know well. Sometimes they are people we think we might like to know." What the student described is definitely voyeuristic but when does it become stalking? A dean of students at a community college said, "A lot more that would be perceived as harassment is going on, but students don't always perceive it as such. Or they articulate it as, 'well, if I took that to be harassing, then 50 percent of the contacts I have would be harassing.'" This situation is exacerbated by the fact that nearly half of the undergraduates surveyed (45 percent) believe they can trust the people they meet through Facebook (Undergraduate Survey, 2009).

A student at church-affiliated university complained, "people just know too much about you before they meet you." The fact of the matter is that a lot of students put a lot of very private information on their Facebook pages—very personal pictures and accounts of intimate experiences. A residence hall counselor said of the residents on her floor, "I think students are pretty open to put anything on Facebook . . . I've seen my residents with forty-ounce bottles taped to their hands. My favorite is when they actually take pictures of themselves doing something stupid."

There are two problems here. One is that students don't comprehend what is public and what is private in digital media. There is a naive sense that communication within the tribe stays within the tribe. Students regularly told us how careful they were with Facebook privacy settings, not realizing, as the dean of a western community college said, "that it's in cyberspace forever and your name is on it." We tell them not to bare "their breasts on Facebook or their rear ends." A colleague lamented that "no matter how much you try to educate them, they still put it all out there on Facebook." Indeed, a number of students interviewed were surprised when they or a friend were confronted by a potential employer with their Facebook profile, were rejected for a job, or were even fired from a job because of their Facebook content. The fact that an employer secured their profile was greeted as almost a magic trick.

The second difficulty is that undergraduates often don't recognize what is inappropriate. Three out of four of the undergraduates surveyed (74 percent) said they would be comfortable with their parents seeing their Facebook site and three out of five (62 percent) said the same about their prospective employers (Undergraduate Survey, 2009). A senior student affairs officer at a highly selective university commented, "You know when we were growing up we knew when to stop. But there's just no stopping with some of the kids in this generation. They just don't know when to stop." In many ways, this is a reaffirmation of the dean who said that current students are rule followers but you have to tell them the rules.

4

Parents

HELICOPTERS, LAWNMOWERS, AND STEALTH BOMBERS

Parents' weekend has become parents' week.
They don't leave.

—VICE PRESIDENT FOR STUDENT AFFAIRS,
SELECTIVE EASTERN UNIVERSITY

I need a launching pad. I have so many
helicopter parents.

—DEAN, SELECTIVE EASTERN COLLEGE

THEY ARE called *helicopter* and *chinook* and *blackhawk* parents because they hover over their children. They are called *lawnmower* and *snowplow* parents because they roll over everything in their paths to "defend" their cubs. They are called *stealth* parents because they swoop in to "protect" their offspring. They are called *umbrella* and *nest* parents because they shield their progeny.

When we interviewed senior student affairs officers and asked what were the most significant changes that have occurred on their campuses since 2001, their overwhelming answer (37 percent) was that parents are more involved. None of the other changes they mentioned came close in frequency. Between 2001 and 2008, three-quarters of all the colleges and universities surveyed reported increases in the frequency of parent involvement and intervention. Half said that the frequency of parent visits had increased. Between 2008 and 2011, seven out ten (68 percent) of the institutions surveyed told us that parent involvement in student lives had increased and a majority (58 percent) reported more parent contacts with administrators and faculty members (Student Affairs Survey, 2008, 2011). As shown in Table 4.1, these phenomena are far more common at four-year schools than at community colleges.

Table 4.1   Percent of Campuses Experiencing Increased Parent Involvement in Student Lives (by Percent)

	Two-year colleges	*Four-year colleges*	*Total*
Increased frequency of parental involvement and intervention since 2001	55	90	76
Increased frequency of parent visits to campus since 2001	32	62	50
Increased frequency of student contact with parents since 2001	34	83	63
Increased parent involvement in student lives since 2008			66
Increased parent contact with faculty members and administration			60

Source: Student Affairs Survey (2008, 2011).

Student affairs officers gave example after example of excessive involvement. These are some of the typical stories, not even the most outlandish:

- "One example, probably not uncommon elsewhere, is when a student was in a discipline conference with our director of residence life. In the middle of the two-way conversation, the student whipped out her cell phone, started talking to her mom, and then handed the phone to a staff member, saying, 'here, talk to my mom.'" [Authors' note: This was indeed not uncommon. We heard stories like this on most of the campuses we visited.]

- "Call from mother: 'My son lost his ID. What should he do?' Response: 'He should get a replacement.' Mother: 'Where does he do that?' Response: 'He should go to the security office.' Mother: 'Where is that?' Response: 'Is your son on campus?' Mother: 'Yes.' Response: 'Tell him to ask someone.'"

- "An RA (resident assistant) gets a call from a parent because it's cold in Johnny's room or facilities gets a call from a parent in Florida because Suzy's stuck in an elevator . . . Facilities asks, 'why didn't Suzy call me? The number's in the elevator.'"

- "A mother . . . called a total of fifteen times one afternoon to reach me, our CFO, and the president to discuss the difficulty her son was having with his wireless Internet connection."

- "We had a parent demand to spend the night with his son in the residence hall for the first week of college. A parent kept calling to see if [her] child was having sex in the residence hall."

- "Just this week, we had a mother e-mail a professor because her son had a dispute with another student in class and the mother wanted to know how we were going to handle the situation. The dean of students' office replied to the mother that we would be contacting her son to discuss the situation and would review his options at that time. The mother e-mailed in return that her son was too busy to meet with us, but she would do so on his behalf."

- A parent complained that the college was not waking up her son to go to class. When the college said they did not do this, the student needed to be self-motivated, the mother responded, "If I thought he could do this on this own, I would have never sent him away to your school and [would have] kept him at home so I could keep doing it for him!" Then she got up and walked out of the office.

- "A parent . . . called asking why we had failed his daughter in class and demanded that she be reinstated and given a passing grade. On investigation, the student had not turned in one assignment, nor passed any tests in the course [in which] she was enrolled."

- A parent wrote, "When you assign roommates, why don't you make sure the parents are a good match as well? I am sending my only child away to college and I want to make sure the other mother is of the same culture I am so we can support each other. I am sure my son's roommate is a very nice young man but I think he's Asian. That will never work; we're from New Jersey."

- "A parent threatened legal action for [a] son not receiving financial aid. The son was twenty-six and had not applied for aid."

- "We had one parent this year who came to her son's room on a regular basis to make sure it was clean."

- We had "parents on campus to move students out of the residence hall without the student even being present."

College Students and Parents

Undergraduates and their parents are in frequent contact. Two out of five students (41 percent) are in touch with parents by phone, e-mail, text, or visit at least daily. One in five (19 percent) is in contact three or more times a day (Undergraduate Survey, 2009). Students who speak with parents frequently told us they like to call between classes to "debrief," "process," "catch up," "get family updates," "ask for money," "say hello," "talk about problems or decisions that need to be made."

The frequency of contact causes several difficulties for campus administrators. First, parents come to expect daily contact, so it's not unusual for administrators to get phone calls from worried parents asking them to check on students who have not called home in a day or two. Second, because students are calling in real time to vent, parents can overreact. One dean at a midwestern liberal arts college said, "It's not unheard of for . . . students to tell parents just how unhappy [they are]. The parents then get alarmed, calls one of us and says, 'Would you check in on my child?' You go and check on this child. [They say], 'What? I'm fine. That was yesterday.' " Third, because children are more likely to contact parents than administrators, parents often know about college problems before the university does. This tends to complicate problems that could have been easily solved.

Students and their parents discuss just about everything, including topics that would have been considered taboo in the past, subjects their parents would have been very unlikely to discuss with their parents. Significant numbers say they always consult their parents before making academic (37 percent) and social decisions (20 percent). At least a third (33 percent) have told their parents intimate details of their lives, about their social and romantic relationships (58 percent) and experiences with alcohol and drugs (34 percent). The differences between two- and four-year colleges were generally small, but varied, sometimes higher at two-year colleges, sometimes at four-year schools (Undergraduate Survey, 2009).

Most undergraduates asked their parents for advice on college matters—roommates and friends, college courses and assignments, majors and careers, and other aspects of college life. At least one in five have gone even further and asked their parents to intervene in problems with professors (27 percent), employers (27 percent), college administrators (21 percent), and roommates (20 percent) (see Tables 4.2 and 4.3) (Undergraduate Survey, 2009).

Some students told us that as they got older, their parents became more like friends than parents. A few even gave us examples of parents acting like friends, though they generally thought it odd and inappropriate. "Parents come to visit kids [at college] on Friday and Saturday and go out and party . . . They're playing flippy cup [a drinking game] with us. Drinking from our bar . . . They want you to teach them beer bongs."

When we spoke with students whose parents had intervened on their behalf, some were embarrassed and said the intervention was not requested and was not wanted, but more frequent were comments like these: "There is a department on campus that I refuse to go into and I want my dad to go with me. They treat me like I'm sixteen years old . . . I'm twenty-two and I am paying your salary to go here and that's when I give my dad a call. He tells me to go and I'm like, 'nope.'" Another student explained, "I pay every cent of my tuition and financial aid refuses to talk with me . . . Well they will talk to me, but they won't help me and then my mom calls and [she gets] everything." Students saw parents as far more powerful and efficacious than they were.

Table 4.2 Percent of Students Asking Advice from Parents on Specific Topics by Institutional Type (by Percent)

	Roommates or friends			College courses or assignments			Majors or careers			Other aspects of college life		
	Two	Four	Total	Two	Four	Total	Two	Four	Total	Two	Four	Total
Never	58	41	49	49	36	42	48	34	40	48	29	37
Once or twice	16	20	18	19	21	20	25	26	26	20	23	22
Used to, but not any more	9	8	9	3	7	5	5	15	10	9	7	8
Few times a year	7	14	11	14	18	16	14	16	15	11	20	16
More than once a month	6	11	9	9	13	11	5	7	6	9	14	12
More than once a week	4	6	5	6	5	5	4	3	3	4	7	6

Note: By two-year institution and four-year institution.

Source: Undergraduate Survey (2009).

Table 4.3 Percent of Students Who Ask Parents to Intervene with Various Campus Constituencies by Institutional Type (by Percent)

	Roommate			Professor			Administrator			Employer		
	Two	Four	Total	Two	Four	Total	Two	Four	Total	Two	Four	Total
Never	91	71	80	77	69	73	81	78	79	72	73	73
Once or twice	2	11	7	9	11	10	10	11	11	14	13	14
Used to, but not any more	2	6	4	2	5	3	3	2	2	4	3	3
Few times a year	4	5	5	8	6	7	5	6	5	5	6	6
More than once a month	1	4	3	2	5	4	3	3	2	3	4	4
More than once a week	1	3	2	3	3	3	1	1	1	1	2	1

Note: By two-year institution and four-year institution.

Source: Undergraduate Survey (2009).

Reasons for Increased Parental Involvement

There is no single reason for the rise in parent involvement in the lives of their children and their colleges. The smartphone is part of the answer. It's easy to stay in touch. It is also the norm for students to start phoning immediately after class and call someone, a member of their tribe. They can text and e-mail in class. Parents are high on the list for many.

Undergraduates are also close to their parents and hold them in higher esteem than their predecessors. When students were asked whether they had heroes, half (51 percent) said yes (Undergraduate Survey, 2009). When asked to name their heroes, they didn't cite celebrities or corporate, government, or social leaders. Less than 1 percent named people like Barack Obama, Martin Luther King Jr., the Dalai Lama, Ronald Reagan, Rosa Parks, Al Gore, Abraham Lincoln, Margaret Thatcher, their teachers, or their professors. They dismissed cultural heroes. Student explained it this way: "With reality TV, you see these people who you might have looked up to just totally trashed and not doing moral enough right things. So why would you want to consider them heroes?" "In terms of cultural heroes . . . it's hard because we don't even see sports stars like that anymore. We don't see politicians. We have a very cynical generation." They saw the faults in these people magnified by the media, which made them unworthy to serve as heroes. "Hero is a cliché." "It's almost like when I think of hero, I think of superhero."

Instead, a majority (54 percent) of undergraduates with heroes named their parents. In total, two-thirds (66 percent) cited a family member. God and Jesus (8 percent) followed distantly behind (Undergraduate Survey, 2009). Students said their heroes were "role models," "mentors," "[people who] had done tremendous things," "someone to look up to." The reasons for choosing parents dealt principally with the sacrifices they made, the opportunities and encouragements they gave their children, and their accomplishments in the world:

- They gave me "unconditional love," "gave me confidence."
- My mother "is an independent woman. Her husband left her with three small children at a very young age. She did not have it exactly easy."
- ". . . single mom. She gave up a lot to make sure I could be where I am."
- My dad "had to go through hard things to give me advantages he didn't have."
- "They have good core values."
- "She's always there."
- "My mom provides for our family and that is kind of who I want to be. I want [that] twenty years or thirty years from now[;] I hope my children say that."
- "She grew up in a time of hatred and married interracially."
- "They sacrificed everything so we could have something."
- "We weren't well off financially and dad hated his job. He overcame a lot of misfortunes and still has a positive upbeat attitude all the time. He just kept true to himself."
- Dad "started with literally nothing and now has everything."
- "She just always, always listens to me, even when I am saying something totally stupid. She listens."

The heroes of today's students are a sharp contrast with their 1993 counterparts. Roughly the same percentage have heroes (55 percent) but who their heroes are has changed dramatically. Whereas parents were the most commonly mentioned heroes in 1993 (29 percent), the proportion of undergraduates who cite their parent now has almost doubled. Deities have declined significantly (15 percent) and public figures—entertainers (6 per-cent), politicians and government leaders (5 percent), and athletes (5 percent) as well as teachers and professors (5 percent)—have fallen off the list (Undergraduate Survey, 1993, 2009). The bot-tom line is that parents have risen in stature over the past two decades in the eyes of their children, which makes them far more likely for students to turn to for counsel and assistance.

A third factor as dean of students after dean of students told us is that today's undergraduates have "a delayed sense of inde-pendence and being a grown up." They have "a very extended adolescence." The dean at an eastern liberal arts college said, "The same way that some people say sixty is the new forty, twenty-one is the new sixteen." "Mature adulthood" is delayed in this genera-tion. "Their mothers make their doctors' appointments and do their laundry and write their papers and . . ." There is "almost an expectation because the parents have been involved so much all through their lives that this is normal for them. They don't really question their parents being involved in their college life, which they are."

Deans frequently described current undergraduates as "very needy." The numbers using psychological counseling services are soaring across the country and students are coming to counseling with deeper and longer-term problems. Between 2001 and 2008, the number of incoming students reporting mental health issues increased at 68 percent of community colleges and 90 percent of the four-year colleges surveyed . Over the next three years, 77 percent of the colleges and universities surveyed had increased use of psychological counseling (Student Affairs Survey, 2008, 2011). The number of students on campus using psychological counsel-ing ranged from 5 to 40 percent at different schools. Psychological counseling staff told us they believed the number of students experiencing severe psychiatric problems will continue to increase, "and the rarity and complexity of their issues will increase [as well]. There will be more of them and they will be more severe."

Use of disability services, including affective, cognitive, and physical support, has also increased at 83 percent of four-year colleges and 72 percent of two-year colleges. Attention deficit disorder was cited as one of the fastest-growing disabilities (Student Affairs Survey, 2008).

This is a generation that has been well protected by their parents, "coddled" as one student newspaper editor stated. The vice president for student affairs at a western research university described "parenting today. We don't want our kids to suffer and so we get involved. So they don't learn how to deal with disappointment and frustration . . . So that when they come to college, when they're hurt, they don't know what to do with it because they have never had to walk through the pain." "We have a big population of students[who] haven't grown up with the coping skills, the problem-solving skills because of the parent involvement growing up." They can't solve their roommate problems and instead turn to their parents because "they don't have the skills that can solve it."

A consequence of the lack of experience with failure and concomitant need to develop coping skills is that this is a generation "who have done very little wrong and made very few mistakes." Current undergraduates have been characterized by several deans as the generation in which "everyone won a trophy or ribbon." They think very well of themselves and believe they are special. The vice president of student affairs for a midwestern regional university characterized current students as "the you generation—you are great, you are wonderful." This has produced a sense of entitlement and a need for constant reaffirmation. A liberal arts college student agreed, stating, "Our generation has this real sense of entitlement. Like our parents were the children of the sixties and seventies and they said I am going to do the best that I can to give my children what they need and what they want and what they deserve." A result is that they are unprepared for stumbles. Even worse, they are surprised when they occur and baffled about how to deal with them. For the dean of a southern liberal arts college the result was a real conundrum. "In terms of holding students accountable and instilling responsibility, that bumped up against a sense of entitlement, [which] gets pretty challenging especially when you have the parents . . . with the same sense of entitlement asking you what in the heck are you doing to my poor Johnny."

A final factor is consumerism. This was a reality in the prior study as well but it has grown in the current study. In a 2009 nationwide poll by the National Center for Public Policy and Higher Education and Public Agenda, 60 percent of respondents believed that colleges and universities are "like most businesses and mainly care about the bottom line," a number which has risen steadily since 2007 versus 32 percent who agreed that institutions of higher education were largely concerned with "making sure students had a good educational experience" (Immerwahr, 2010, p. 2). A student at a Pacific Coast university captured the statistics when he said, "In general, it seems like the college campuses, especially this one, is more concerned with profits, how much money they can get from their students. The education system just seems to be going more towards a purely business standpoint rather than being here for the students."

Deans reported that parents and students behaved increasingly like consumers and treated colleges as they would businesses. A Pacific coast vice president for student affairs said they act as if "they are the customer and it's kind of I'm paying for this so I'm entitled to this. I actually had a student tell me that because they paid for it and they were going to class, they deserved an A." A western research university peer agreed, saying parents have shifted the sense of higher education from the educational mission to a consumer model . . . I think it's easier for them to think about us as a hotel or business." As one would call the supermarket, the cable company, or the bank to complain about poor service, parents and students are increasingly treating colleges in the same fashion. The fact is that they are paying high prices, which are commonly rising more quickly than inflation. There is an expectation that as prices increase, so should product quality. And half of the undergraduates surveyed are not happy with the way in which they are being treated. They do not believe colleges are "giving adequate respect to the people paying tuition" (Undergraduate Survey, 2009).

Students complained not infrequently about poor customer service—courses being unavailable, "bureaucracy," inaccurate information, inability to get information, being sent from office to office, and the like. Deans countered that this generation asks questions, wants to be told what to do rather than trying to figure out the answers themselves. To some extent, students and their parents are responding to institutions of higher education the same way they would to other businesses that they felt had not served them well. At least one out of every eight colleges surveyed experienced parent grievances against faculty members (19 percent) or staff (13 percent) or were taken to court by parents or students (13 percent) in the past year (Student Affairs Survey, 2008).

Parent involvement in higher education does not appear to be a quickly passing fad. For a decade, institutions have reported continuing increases in parent involvement in college affairs and their children's lives. Digital devices, which serve as electronic umbilical cords, are staples in the diphobe campus culture. For more than a quarter of students, their parents are their heroes. And the consumer attitude regarding college is likely to grow as long as the prices keep rising. In any case, colleges are not acting as if they expect parent involvement to diminish soon. One college was talking seriously of creating a dean of parents' position. Another laughingly said they had the equivalent of bouncers at orientation to shoo parents away. Parent newsletters, e-mail blasts, and parallel and joint events for parents and their children, such as career fairs, are increasingly common. The same is becoming true in the workplace. As the phone call volume increased, one major investment bank went so far as to institute a parents' day to orient the moms and dads of new hires to the workplace and its expectations.

5

Multiculturalism

THE DEMOGRAPHICS OF COMFORT

My generation crossed the religious barrier. My children's generation will cross the racial barrier.

—BABY BOOMER PARENT

WHEN *HOPE* and *Fear Collide* reported that diversity was the most heated issue on the nation's college campuses; there were deep divides between undergraduates of different races. It was a painful subject that students did not want to talk about except in homogeneous racial groups. Racial minorities talked about feeling uncomfortable on campus—"like an unwelcome guest at a party rather than a member of the family" (Levine & Cureton, 1998, p. 73). They spoke of being seen only through the lens of race. "In my classes," said one student, "I am always being asked how African Americans view this or that. I'm not the universal African American but just one person being forced into a very small box." Students of color complained of being stereotyped. A black student from one of the wealthiest suburbs in America said she was asked several times what it was like to grow up in a ghetto. A common complaint was that white students often mixed up people of color, calling them by each others' names, even though they looked nothing alike, thereby giving the impression that whites classified students of color principally by their race.

Among white students, attitudes about race varied by 180 degrees from rejection of the legitimacy of minority concerns, as shown in the attitude of "we already had the civil rights movement," to a tremendous sense of guilt. The dominant feelings, however, were confusion and uncertainty.

Multicultural tensions were high—extending across race, gender, religion, ethnicity, and sexual orientation. They could be seen in college hiring and admissions practices, their academic offerings and campus events, and social and residential life. The dirty words on campus were no longer four letters but had become at least six: *racist, sexist,* and *homophobic.*

The tensions were attributed to four causes. The first was a preoccupation with differences on the part of students. Undergraduates tended to think of themselves in terms of the characteristics that made them unique—race, gender, ethnicity, sexual orientation, geography, and religion rather than the commonalties they shared. By contrast, the students of the 1970s focused on their shared generational characteristics—being career oriented, wanting material success, being politically disinterested, and caring about their appearance

The second cause of tension, which really flows from the first, was the mitosis of student groups. The result, for example, is that student clubs kept getting smaller and more specialized. The undergraduate business and entrepreneurship club might divide into Asian, black, women's, gay, Caribbean, Catholic, and accounting business clubs. In turn, the Asian business club might break into Chinese, Japanese, southeast Asian, and Korean business clubs. In this manner, undergraduates continually reduced the number of students they defined as being like themselves.

Self-segregation was a third cause. That is, if one walked into the college cafeteria, one would have seen black students sitting with other blacks, whites with whites, Asians with Asians, and Hispanics with Hispanics. The larger an institution's enrollment, the more differentiated the separate groups tended to become. For instance, at universities enrolling tens of thousands of students, the Hispanic table was likely replaced by separate tables for Dominicans, Mexicans, Puerto Ricans, and Columbians. There was also a tendency at many colleges for particular student groups to take possession of specific locations on campus—a lounge, a place in the cafeteria, the student union, or the library—by virtue of squatters rights.

The final element was a sense of victimization, the belief that I or students like me were being disadvantaged to the benefit of others. The others were getting more financial aid, more resources from the student government, superior jobs on campus, greater coverage in the curriculum, less harsh treatment by the disciplinary committee, better campus facilities, or enhanced student services—just about anything.

Multiculturalism on Campus Today

Colleges and universities seem very different places today. The multicultural divide is less deep; the gap between diverse groups is less wide. The changes are not apparent in the statistics. The level of racial and religious tension has remained constant at the vast majority of colleges and universities with rough parity between institutions experiencing increases and declines since 2001. Student affairs officers tended to minimize religious tensions, saying that any incidents that had occurred were largely in response to September 11 and seemed to have faded but not disappeared over time.

Hate incidents involving race, sexual orientation, or religion, which were very rare on the campuses we visited, have also held steady at most institutions though declines slightly outnumbered increases (see Table 5.1). There also continue to be the personal daily frictions attributed to multicultural differences, which occur in any location

Table 5.1 Multicultural Tension and Hate Incidents by Institutional Type and Percent Experiencing

	Decreased			Remained the same			Increased		
	Two year	Four year	Total	Two year	Four year	Total	Two year	Four year	Total
Racial tension 2001–2008	8	9	11	88	75	80	5	12	9
Racial tension 2008–2011			13			70			17
Religious tension 2001–2008	5	9	8	92	78	84	3	13	9
Religious tension 2008–2011			5			86			10
Hate incidents involving race 2001–2008	11	17	14	82	78	80	8	5	6
Hate incidents involving sexual orientation 2001–2008	6	17	12	83	78	80	11	5	8
Hate incidents involving religion 2001–2008	6	9	8	94	88	90	3	2

Source: Student Affairs Survey (2008, 2011).

where people interact at a college—from the dormitories, administrative offices, and libraries to bookstores, classrooms, and playing fields.

The tensions and incidents that do occur are exacerbated by a lack of historical context and understanding on the part of students today. Actions, words, and symbols laden with historic meaning are sometimes trotted out unknowingly by students and provoke strong reactions. A noose was mentioned on several campuses. The use of one group's slang by members of another group has also been problematic, even when applied strictly to members of the other group if overheard. The most frequent examples were the use of words such as *bitch* and *nigger*, which are fairly common in popular music these days. Talking "ghetto," which has been picked up by white students, is a potent source of discord.

Complicating this is the fact that students, majorities and minorities alike, in a generation weak in interpersonal skills, also seek to avoid discussing diversity issues, according to many student affairs staff. There is more smoldering and less conversation. Political correctness is another bar to conversation. In 1992, three out of five student affairs officers characterized their campus climate as politically correct. In the current study, a quarter of campuses reported increases in political correctness since 2001 (Student Affairs Survey, 1992, 2008). Diversity problems are one of the topics most frequently left for parents to raise with the dean.

There is also still voluntary segregation by race and to a lesser extent by religion. More than two of every five white (44 percent), black (43 percent), and Hispanic (45 percent) students as well as a majority of Asian American undergraduates (51 percent) report that on their campuses students of different racial and ethnic groups pretty much keep to themselves. Half or more of the students surveyed—whites (77 percent), blacks (53 percent), Hispanics (50 percent), and Asian Americans (57 percent)—say they primarily socialize with members of their own race whether they mean to or not (Undergraduate Survey, 2009). And at nearly half of the nation's colleges and universities (47 percent), there continue to be campus locations that belong to specific racial, ethnic, or religious groups, more at four-year colleges (52 percent) than community colleges (40 percent). Undergraduates still believe that other students on campus are being offered advantages they are not. In fact, compared to 1993 that feeling has grown among men (30 percent in 1993 versus 40 percent in 2009), women (31 percent versus 37 percent), whites (31 percent versus 33 percent), blacks (36 percent versus 37 percent), Hispanics (33 percent versus 52 percent), and Asians (42 percent versus 56 percent) (Undergraduate Survey, 1993, 2009).

There has also been an expansion in the number of campus clubs and organizations dedicated to specific ethnic, racial, gender, sexual orientation, and religious populations. We call them *student affinity group* (see Table 5.2).

Table 5.2 Percent of Institutions with Various Affinity Groups by Year

	1969	1978	1992	1997	2008
African American	46	58	68	55	63
Women	27	48	49	51	61
Hispanic	13	22	41	43	53
Native American	6	13	21	27	21
Gay, lesbian, bisexual, transgendered	2	11	35	40	60
International			69	68	67
Disabilities			35	32	22
Asian American			34	36	43
Multicultural umbrella			32	31	52
Men			21	14	53
Arab American					20

Source: Student Affairs Survey (1978, 1992, 1997, 2008); Undergraduate Survey (1969).

What Changed?

The most important changes are that students of different races, ethnicities, and genders are more satisfied with their college experience. Their attitudes on race and gender issues have become much less polarized. And there is a greater sense of opportunity and progress for diverse populations.

Students Are More Satisfied with College

Female, male, white, black, Hispanic, and Asian American students are more positive about their college experience. They feel a greater sense of community. They are more satisfied with the quality of the teaching. They are more likely to have professors whom they can turn to for personal advice and who take a special interest in their academic progress. More believe students at their school are comfortable expressing unpopular and controversial positions (see Table 5.3).

Polarization Among Different Racial and Ethnic Groups on Issues of Race Has Declined

Attitudes about race, racial discrimination, conditions on campus, and relationships between races have converged and grown more positive among undergraduates, which serves to diminish the divide found in the prior study. People of color are more likely to believe that the country has made racial gains and a number of initiatives necessary to protect against discrimination are less needed today. A majority of whites are likely to think that there needs to be greater diversity on campus and affirmative action continues to be necessary. Large majorities of whites and undergraduates of color have close friends of other races and support intergroup relationships.

In contrast to the 1993 Undergraduate Survey, white, black, Hispanic, and Asian American students are now more likely to

Table 5.3 Satisfaction with College by Gender and Race (by Percent)

	Female		Male		Whites		Blacks		Hispanics		Asians	
	1993	2009	1993	2009	1993	2009	1993	2009	1993	2009	1993	2009
I feel a sense of community at this institution.	64	80	66	70	63	86	59	72	64	87	58	67
Overall satisfied with teaching	83	87	80	85	82	86	80	87	80	82	75	88
I have professors I can turn to for personal advice.	54	62	80	85	53	61	44	80	52	53	47	56
I have professors who take a special interest in my academic progress.	67	77	63	76	67	82	63	75	66	80	45	61

Source: Undergraduate Survey (1993, 2009).

think the country has made real progress toward racial equality in the past five years. They are less likely to believe racial discrimination will hurt their job chances, ethnic studies programs should be controlled by people of that ethnic group, more minority students should be admitted even if it requires different admission standards, and more is heard about the rights of minorities and not enough about the rights of majorities.

A majority of undergraduates report that they have a close friend of a different race, believe that undergraduate education would be improved if there were greater diversity in students and faculty, and think their colleges have diverse student bodies. Similarly, only a minority of students say they are more comfortable socializing with people of their own race, professors at their colleges do not take minority students seriously, and they are uncomfortable with interracial dating and marriage.

At higher rates than in 1993, whites, blacks, and Hispanics reject the idea that most American colleges are racist whether they mean to be or not. Asian American opinion has not changed. Whites and blacks are more likely today to say that people on their campuses feel comfortable expressing unpopular and controversial positions. A majority of Hispanics and Asian Americans concur but at lower rates than in 1993 (see Table 5.4).

The sharpest areas of disagreement among students deal with life after college, what employment policy should be, and what job practices are in today's difficult economy. Large majorities of blacks and Hispanics believe that minorities with the same qualifications should be given preference for jobs over nonminorities, and minorities have to be twice as good as majority group members to get ahead. Whites and Asian Americans disagree.

Females Believe Opportunity for Women Has Improved

Changes of opinion regarding gender are very similar to those on ethnicity and race. Most women believe that the United States has

Table 5.4 Attitudes Regarding Multicultural Issues by Race (by Percent)

	Whites		Blacks		Hispanics		Asian Americans	
	1993	2009	1993	2009	1993	2009	1993	2009
The country has not made real progress toward racial equality in last five years.	47	34	75	66	55	38	58	40
Racial discrimination will hurt my job chances.	8	4	67	36	28	20	53	29
Ethnic studies programs should be administered and controlled by people of that ethnic group.	48	44	70	44	61	52	57	24
More minority groups should be admitted to my college even if it means using different admissions criteria.	25	21	55	42	48	38	43	21
We hear more about the rights of minorities and not enough about the majority.	60	66	13	41	40	59	34	35
I have at least one close friend of a different race.		81		69		84		81
Undergraduate education would be improved if there were greater diversity in students.		54		75		57		73
Undergraduate education would be improved if there were greater diversity in the faculty.		50		79		57		66

Statement							
Affirmative action is no longer necessary.				45	37	45	48
My college has a diverse student body.				69	66	85	84
I am more comfortable socializing with people of my own race.				40	34	36	45
Professors at my college do not take minority students seriously.				6	26	27	12
I am not comfortable with interracial dating and marriage.				21	24	18	29
Most American colleges are racist whether they mean to be or not.		31	20	57	26	37	45	45
People at my school feel comfortable expressing unpopular and controversial positions.	65	71	61	70	65	51	66	56
Racial and ethnic minorities should be given preference for jobs if they have the same qualifications as nonminority applicants.				29	78	75	34
To get ahead minorities (racial and ethnic) have to be twice as good as majorities.				28	78	68	37

Source: Undergraduate Survey (1993, 2009).

made real progress toward gender equity in the last five years. They reject the notions that American colleges are sexist whether they want to be or not and that their professors do not take women seriously. They are also less likely to think sexual discrimination will hurt their employment chances or that women have to be twice as good as men to get a job. More think women in the armed forces should be permitted to serve in combat positions. More women (45 percent versus 38 percent) and men (32 percent versus 23 percent) than in 1993 believe that females should be given preference for jobs if they have the same qualifications as male applicants, though still only minorities of each hold this opinion. Three out of five women (61 percent) and men (59 percent) surveyed also think feminism has not become an outdated idea, though the term was often described as shrill and of another era (see Table 5.5).

Table 5.5   Women's Attitudes on Gender by Year (by Percent)

	1993	2009
The country has not made real progress toward gender equity in the last five years.		44
Most of America's colleges and universities are sexist whether they want to be or not.		19
Professors at my school do not really take women students seriously.	11	9
Sexual discrimination will hurt my job chances.	36	17
To get ahead in this world, a woman has to be twice as good at what she does as a man at what he does.	70	33
Women in the armed forces should not be permitted to serve in combat positions.	28	22

Source: Undergraduate Survey (1993, 2009).

What Caused the Change?

Part of the answer is that the demographics of the nation have changed as discussed in Chapter One and higher education has followed suit. As noted, the students on US campuses are the most diverse generation in higher education history. Most four-year colleges surveyed reported increased racial and ethnic, socioeconomic, biracial, and language diversity. Nearly half said the number of gay, lesbian, bisexual, and transgendered students had grown. Community colleges also experienced significant growth but at lower levels (see Table 5.6). This means students on most campuses see and interact by choice or circumstance with more people who are different than they are, and groups that were once smaller have achieved sufficient numbers to provide a comfort zone for members on campus.

There is more homogeneity between groups and greater heterogeneity within diverse groups than in the past as well.

Greater Homogeneity Among Ethnic, Racial, and Gender Groups

When Hope and Fear Collide described a generation in which college students of differing races, ethnicities, and genders grew up

---

Table 5.6   Increases in Diversity by Group and Institutional Type (by Percent)

	Two-year colleges	Four-year colleges	Total
Racial and ethnic diversity	59	75	68
Socioeconomic diversity	43	57	52
Biracial diversity	45	60	54
Multilingual diversity	51	58	55
Gay, lesbian, bisexual, and transgendered diversity	31	49	42

Source: Student Affairs Survey (2008).

in almost separate worlds. The key events that shaped their lives were different. The personalities they viewed positively and negatively were often mirror images. For example, the undergraduates surveyed in 1993 were given a list of twenty-six well-known personalities in politics, sports, and entertainment and asked to rate them positively or negatively. When the ratings of blacks and whites were compared, three of five individuals blacks rated most positively—Malcolm X, Spike Lee, and Jesse Jackson—were on the list whites rated most negatively, and two of the five people whites rated most highly—Ross Perot and Boris Yeltsin—were on the most negative list for blacks (Levine & Cureton, 1998).

This is no longer the case. In this generation, the worlds in which diverse groups of undergraduates grew up were in many respects more alike than separate. The key events that shaped their lives were generally the same—the advent of the World Wide Web, web browsers, and digital devices; the poor economy, the election of Barack Obama, and September 11. The only difference was the order in which they cited these events and that black students alone chose the civil rights movement as more important in their lives than the September 11 attacks. Asian Americans added the subprime mortgage crisis and blacks mentioned the presidential campaign of Hillary Clinton and Hurricane Katrina. These items were on their peers' lists as well, just lower in priority (see Table 5.7).

The people who loomed large in the worlds of diverse groups, positively and negatively, were almost identical. The polar nature of the 1993 assessments for different ethnic and racial groups was gone in the most recent undergraduate survey. Asked to rate a list of forty-eight prominent figures from across the country and around the world, college students gave their most positive rankings to Bill Gates, Barack Obama, Bill Clinton, Al Gore, and Angelina Jolie. Nelson Mandela, Hilary Clinton, Ronald Reagan, Joseph Biden, and Ted Kennedy were also evaluated positively

Table 5.7 The Six Key Events Most Cited by Undergraduates by Race and Gender (by Percent)

Women	Men	Asians	Blacks	Hispanics	Whites
Advent of World Wide Web	Advent of World Wide Web	Advent of World Wide Web	Obama election	Economic downturn and rising gas prices	Advent of World Wide Web
Economic downturn and rising gas prices	Economic downturn and rising gas prices	Advent of Yahoo! and Google	Advent of World Wide Web	Advent of World Wide Web	Economic downturn and rising gas prices
September 11 attack	September 11 attack	Economic downturn and rising gas prices	Economic downturn and rising gas prices	September 11 attack	September 11 attack
Obama election	Obama election	September 11 attack	Civil rights movement	Obama election	Launch of cell phone
Launch of cell phone	Launch of cell phone	Subprime mortgage crisis	Hilary Clinton presidential run	Advent of Yahoo! and Google	Obama election; advent of Yahoo! and Google
Advent of Yahoo! and Google	Advent of Yahoo! and Google	Advent of cell phone	Hurricane Katrina	Launch of cell phone	

Source: Undergraduate Survey (2009).

by students and frequently appeared on their top-seven lists. The most negatively rated were almost universal—Paris Hilton, Fidel Castro, 50 Cent, George Bush, Dick Cheney, and Monica Lewinsky. Sarah Palin and Amy Winehouse found their way onto some group negative lists, too (see Table 5.8).

There were people who straddled the lists. In the last undergraduate survey, Jessie Jackson was a prime example, appearing on the black top positive list and the white top negative list. He remained a controversial figure in this survey as well but assessments of him were much more moderate. The dramatic polarity was gone. Blacks rated him positively but not sufficiently to make their most positive list. Whites and Hispanics gave him negatives that were very slightly higher than his positives.

Ronald Reagan was not called the Teflon president for nothing. He made the transition from the black most negative ratings to their positive list and rose in the rankings of all other groups, too. As with the assessments in 1993, the ratings in the current version were not ideological. Undergraduates gave high positive ratings to an odd assortment of people—Ronald Reagan and Ted Kennedy, for example. The most frequent rationale for their top positive choices was that these people made the world a better place or succeeded in a difficult struggle. This is reminiscent of the personal reasons students gave for choosing their parents as heroes.

The negative lists of students were even more eclectic. There was little that tied the members together. Bush and Cheney received their rankings for the wars and the economy. Fidel Castro was selected because he was a totalitarian ruler. The message and lifestyles of 50 Cent and the late Amy Winehouse were criticized. Paris Hilton and Monica Lewinsky were seen as self-absorbed, irresponsible, and bad role models for girls. It is interesting that Bill Clinton made the students' top-seven positive list and Monica Lewinsky was placed in their bottom seven.

Table 5.8 Personalities Perceived as Most Positive and Most Negative by Race and Gender of Respondent (by Percent)

Perceived Most Negative

Women	Men	Asians	Blacks	Hispanics	Whites
Paris Hilton	Fidel Castro	Paris Hilton	George W. Bush	Paris Hilton	Paris Hilton
Monica Lewinsky	Paris Hilton	Fidel Castro	Fidel Castro	Amy Winehouse	Fidel Castro
Fidel Castro	Monica Lewinsky	George W. Bush	Monica Lewinsky	50 Cent	Monica Lewinsky
Amy Winehouse	Amy Winehouse	50 Cent	Paris Hilton	Fidel Castro	Amy Winehouse
George W. Bush	50 Cent	Monica Lewinsky	Dick Cheney	Monica Lewinsky	50 Cent
50 Cent	Dick Cheney	Dick Cheney	Sarah Palin	George W. Bush	Dick Cheney
Dick Cheney	George W. Bush	Sarah Palin	50 Cent	Dick Cheney	Sarah Palin

Perceived Most Positive

Women	Men	Asians	Blacks	Hispanics	Whites
Bill Gates	Bill Gates	Bill Gates	Barack Obama	Bill Gates	Bill Gates
Barack Obama	Barack Obama	Barack Obama	Bill Gates	Barack Obama and Bill Clinton	Barack Obama
Nelson Mandela	Ronald Reagan	Bill Clinton	Bill Clinton	Hillary Clinton	Ronald Reagan
Al Gore	Al Gore	Angelina Jolie	Hillary Clinton	Ted Kennedy	Al Gore
Bill Clinton and Ronald Reagan	Hillary Clinton	Hillary Clinton	Nelson Mandela	Joe Biden	Bill Clinton
Angelina Jolie	Bill Clinton and Angelina Jolie	Al Gore	Al Gore	Ronald Reagan	Angelina Jolie
	Ronald Reagan	Ronald Reagan	Angelina Jolie		Joe Biden and John McCain

Source: Undergraduate Survey (2009).

Also worthy of note is who was not mentioned. The list of names students were given included people such as the late Kim Jung Il of North Korea and Mahmoud Ahmadinejad of Iran. But most students did not recognize those names or many others as noted in Chapter One. A third or more did not know the names of such domestic figures as comedian Jon Stewart (34 percent), Supreme Court Chief Justice John Roberts (66 percent), radio commentator Rush Limbaugh (36 percent), and former speaker of the House of Representatives Nancy Pelosi (37 percent) (Undergraduate Survey, 2009).

The good news is that the list also included one made-up name, which was intended to be perceived as mideastern. We feared students would rate him negatively in the current War on Terror climate. However, more than four out of five students (81 percent) said they did not recognize the name. But the few who rated him were slightly more negative than positive (Undergraduate Survey, 1993, 2009).

This is the post–*Cosby Show* generation. Today's college students grew up in a time in which the media no longer portrayed people of color wholly as maids, sports stars, and service employees and all women were not housewives or working in the traditional female jobs. Instead women and people of color were heads of major companies; ran for the highest offices in the land; served on the Supreme Court; were governors, legislators, and mayors; hosted or starred in network and cable television shows; became public intellectuals; and lived in the White House. Though America remains highly segregated by race, ethnicity, geography, and income, many, many college students told us while they were growing up they had continuing contact with people of different ethnicities and races. Not only did they see them in the media, they may have gone to school together, played together, socialized in mixed groups, lived on the same block, worked together or depended on them for professional services. Boys and girls socialized in groups. And the Internet where they spent a great deal of time was color blind. In any case, for most students "they" were not strangers or aliens when they met each other in college, though this was certainly the case for some.

Greater Diversity Within Groups

At the same time, the composition of ethnic, racial, and gender groups on campus changed. The vice president at a western research university told us "there is more diversity of the diverse students who are coming." Though of the same ethnicity or race, students arrive on campus today more than in the past from different income strata, geographies, social classes, family experiences, educational backgrounds, and interests. They are first-generation college students and multigenerational attendees, rich and poor, taking remedial classes and having piles of Advanced Placement credits, from the inner cities and the most affluent suburbs, and needing full scholarships and paying full sticker price. The fact that they share a common skin color is often not sufficient to overcome their differences.

Students reported feeling they were not part of their racial or ethnic group. Mexican students on one campus in the West talked of a split between natives and immigrants. Natives were accused of not being Mexican enough. Another student from Mexico in a focus group talked about cultural differences with regard to dress. "If you cross the border every single day, you tend to dress up every single day, whereas people who live in El Paso can very well come in pjs to school." She saw the two populations as fundamentally different. A black student at an eastern liberal arts college talked of being called *white* by other African Americans because of his lack of familiarity with their culture, his dating habits, and his dress. A student at Pacific Coast research university spoke of yet a different variety of fit. "A lot of people look at me and don't label me as Chicano but I can speak Spanish. My mom is from Mexico and my dad is from Ecuador, but in high school [in a very diverse community], I just hung out with so many different people from all different backgrounds that I wanted a diverse group of friends, not just Latinos." The bottom line is that although there are aggregations of students of the same race and ethnicity in dining rooms at the nation's colleges, there are in the words of one liberal arts college dean "students of color scattered all over the place."

Biracial students who are increasing in number are a special case. An undergraduate who was black, Asian, and lesbian said she didn't feel like she belonged anywhere. These characteristics were all parts of who she was and she felt a number of groups wanted her to choose one. At one college, they referred to these students as *TCKs*, third culture kids. Many biracial undergraduates were having a hard time trying to figure out who they were in a society that tends to classify people by single attributes and what their relationships and affiliations should be on campus. However, as their numbers continue to increase, one dean told us, they will find greater comfort in achieving a critical mass and be a force for breaking down the traditional divisions on campus.

Another element is that new identities are springing up that cross the racial, ethnic, and gender boundaries. When asked what diversity issue caused the greatest tension on campus, equal numbers of deans said race and sexual orientation. When asked which were the most activist groups on campus, gay, lesbian, bisexual, and transgendered (GBLT) organizations were most frequently cited. This is not surprising because the issue of gay rights has been superheated in this nation in recent years. There were government actions that advanced gay rights and others that restricted them. The year the class of 2015 was born, the Clinton administration circumvented the ban on gays in the military by adopting the "don't ask, don't tell" policy, barring the military from asking members about their sexual orientation. Eighteen years later, the ban on gays in the military was lifted, but Washington drew a line at gay marriage with the Defense of Marriage Act when the class of 2015 was thirteen. However, when they were eleven, Massachusetts became the first state to legalize same-sex marriage, setting off an avalanche of state referenda and legislative and court actions around the country.

Similar to the civil rights issues dealing with race and gender that preceded it, the GBLT rights debate has come to the nation's campuses, where two-thirds (65 percent) of undergraduates support gay dating and marriage and civil unions, slightly more at four-year schools (68) than community colleges (61 percent) (Undergraduate Survey, 2009). Colleges and universities and the young people who attend them will serve as a crucible for debate, study, and activism.

Another diversity issue boiling on many campuses is social class, which was spotlighted by the 2011 Occupy Campus movement, an outshoot of Occupy Wall Street. Social class was described as a potentially more powerful issue than race, ethnicity, or gender because it builds on the current heterogeneity and cracks within those communities. One student newspaper editor believed social class would overtake race as the greatest diversity issue in the near future. Certainly, it is far more prominent in the national political debate today. Rising levels of activism regarding social class and sexual orientation are discussed in Chapter Six.

For all of the reasons enumerated and perhaps others as well, the simple fact is that there is more interaction among diverse groups on campus. There is, according to deans, more interracial and GBLT dating as well as more interracial and interethnic socializing. Even the acts that were considered deeply troubling in the last study are considered more benign or even positive. For instance, although there is even greater mitosis or division of student groups based on identity differences, deans say it is doing more today to enrich than detract from campus life (see Table 5.9). There continues to be self-segregation on campuses by race and ethnicity, but it is more often seen by peers and student affairs staffers as a vehicle for students to find comfort than a sign of racial or ethnic schism.

Table 5.9 Perceptions of Multicultural Practices on Campus by Institutional Type (by Percent)

	Two-year colleges	Four-year colleges	Total
Increased frequency of interracial dating	22	37	31
Increased frequency of GLBT dating	17	41	31
Increased frequency of interracial and inter-ethnic socializing	29	45	39
Increased frequency of interfaith socializing	12	37	28
Increased enrichment of campus life resulting from multiplication or division of groups based on identity differences	29	44	38
Increased problems in campus life resulting from multiplication or division of groups based on identity differences	15	20	18

Source: Student Affairs Survey (2008).

What has truly happened is that the zone of indifference, the degree to which actions are ignored or little import or meaning is ascribed to them, quite small in the previous study, is larger today. Differences of all sorts are a fact of life for current college students, characterized by one dean as a race-blind generation and by many others as "more comfortable with" or more accepting of difference. The latter seems a more accurate description of campuses in which racial, ethnic, and gender tensions continue but the divisions are of lesser dimension. A dean summarized the situation well, saying, "intergroup collaborations and cooperation have increased. [There is] increasing ease in moving across boundaries. We have had in general a lessening of tension across groups. Of course, campuses are always one incident away from going down in flames" (Student Affairs Survey, 2011).

6

Politics

TALKING GLOBAL, ACTING LOCAL

We want change.

—STUDENT

THIS IS a generation of students with less interest in college governance and campus activism than their predecessors. They are disenchanted with politics, politicians, and government and want change. Ideologies—left, right, and center—do not appeal to most of them; rather, they are issue oriented and the issues are personal. When they act, which is often, their theater of action tends to be local, though they often believe the issues that engage them have global implications. However, they have little concrete knowledge about the world.

On-Campus Politics

The relatively low level of student involvement in campus life is also mirrored in their on-campus political interest and engagement. Continuing a trend begun in the 1970s, undergraduates want to be less engaged in college and university governance than their predecessors. Fewer want control or voting power over bachelor degree requirements, faculty hiring and promotion, residence hall regulations, student discipline, and undergraduate admissions requirements. The number who want little or no role in these areas has risen as shown in Table 6.1.

There were stark differences between four- and two-year college enrollees, though the trend was in the same direction. In each governance area, four-year students wanted control and voting power by one to twenty percentage points more than their community college peers (Undergraduate Survey, 1993, 2009).

The one exception is undergraduates seeking a diminished governance role in determining course offerings and content, which students tend to see more as a consumer than a governance issue, that is, ensuring that the classes they need to graduate are

Table 6.1   Student Beliefs About the Roles Undergraduates Should Play in Various Campus Decisions (by Percent)

	Voting Power or Control			*Little or No Role*		
	1976	*1993*	*2009*	*1976*	*1993*	*2009*
Bachelor's degree requirements	25	24	23	21	18	22
Faculty hiring and promotion	29	29	18	22	20	37
Residence hall regulations	70	63	47	5	6	12
Student discipline	64	52	36	6	9	20
Undergraduate admissions requirements	27	24	19	24	22	29
Course offerings and content	32	33	39	10	10	10

Source: Undergraduate Survey (1976, 1993, 2009).

offered in the appropriate sequence, number, and schedule and the content is up-to-date and germane to their future lives and careers. Here the percentage of students who want voting power or control actually increased slightly but still stands at fewer than two out of five undergraduates (39 percent) and the proportion who want little or no control has remained constant.

Student engagement in campus protest activities is also down. This number has oscillated over time. In 1969, the peak for involvement, 28 percent of undergraduates said they had participated in a campus demonstration, protest march, sit-in, or advocacy event. This number dropped to 19 percent in 1976, increased to 25 percent in 1993, and in the most recent survey hit a low of 11 percent (Undergraduate Survey, 1969, 1976, 1993, 2009).

Part of the reason is that student protest tactics have changed dramatically since the surveys began. The 1960s approaches of mass demonstrations, building takeovers, threats of violence, and strikes are largely gone. In fact, protest activities by parents now occur more frequently than any of these. Down too are the tactics that gained popularity in the 1980s and 1990s—taking issues public via press, publications, and mail as well as going to court to seek remedies, as shown in Table 6.2.

Instead, today's protest activities are more individual than group efforts, more impersonal, less risky, and make increasing use of the digital media—e-mail, Internet, and blogs—which were either not available in the earlier studies or not as popular as they are today. Nonetheless, the protest method of choice for students is filing grievances against faculty members and staff, followed by e-mail activism and parent grievances.

It is important to note that only half of all colleges and universities reported experiencing any of these protest activities in the prior year. If grievances are removed, the number drops off by a quarter (Student Affairs Survey, 2008).

Table 6.2   Percent of Campuses Reporting Various Tactics of Student Protest by Year

	1969	1978	1992	1997	2008
Protesting via demonstrations	39	13	33	34	14
Protesting by threats of violence	20	3.	15	22	16
Protesting by taking over building	15		6	3	1
Protesting via strike	14	1	2		
Protesting by intentional destruction of property	12	1	4	5	1
Protesting by taking issue to court	4	6	10	15	13
Protesting by taking issue public via press, publications, mail			27	36	16
Protesting by taking issue public via e-mail				16	25
Protesting by taking issue public via blog					10
Protesting by taking issue public via Internet					19
Protesting by students filing grievances against faculty members					50
Protesting by students filing grievances against staff					30
Protesting by parents filing grievances against faculty					19
Protesting by parents filing grievances against staff					16

Source: Student Affairs Survey (1978 [source of 1969 data], 1992, 1997, 2008).

Student affairs staff, particularly at community colleges and largely commuter four-year institutions, told us one of the major reasons for the lack of activism is that in the current economy students don't have the time. As with participation in out-of-class activities, they have higher and more urgent priorities, such as "the price of heating oil and feeding families." "It is either put food on the table for your family or go to a march."

Apathy was another reason offered to explain low participation rates. This is nothing new. Apathy was mentioned every time this study has been done. On campus after campus, deans said, "our campus tends to be fairly apathetic in terms of political activism." When there were demonstrations, it was not unusual for the numbers participating to be few. Anecdotes were plentiful. Typical was the southern liberal arts schools where a demonstration drew fifty people, which was very large for that campus, but the crowd consisted principally of local community members, and the Pacific Coast university, where a much publicized demonstration turned out to be "three girls yelling into a megaphone."

Beyond apathy, there was a sense that each of the multiple groups on campus had its own issues. One Midwest community college dean described the situation this way: "There is no protest walking through the halls. There is no constant berating over this issue or this has to be changed. Every group is pretty much focused on what's important to them." At an East Coast liberal arts school a student added, "I think definitely different issues are concerns of different groups . . . a lot of activism is done by very small, very powerful groups of students on campus. Powerful not in a negative way; powerful in that they're passionate about what they are doing and they have a huge impact on campus." On the Pacific Coast, a student newspaper editor summarized the state of activism on her campus: "I think it varies so widely based upon which student you are." For her, it came down to the politics of individual concerns.

There was also a belief that students were waiting for someone else to step up and do it. A midwestern student newspaper editor said his classmates "put up a big stink" about an issue and when "it doesn't have the spotlight," they shrug and say "someone else will do it." Another student made the same point a bit more colloquially: "more people bitch than care."

Many deans chalked up the lack of involvement to current students not being risk takers. They are afraid of getting into trouble if they protest. One illustrated with the story of a student who came to see him to ask exactly that question: would he get into trouble if participated in a demonstration? The dean laughed and said, "Isn't that part of protesting, that you are so alarmed that you are willing to pay a cost?" He concluded, "this generation doesn't want to push it too far."

"A lot of them will not act unless they have the approval of an authority figure," said a colleague. As a group, today's undergraduates were described as "sweet," "young," "willing to talk with adults," "polite," "want[ing] to be told what to do," and "always wanting explicit instructions on limits." The students of the 1990s were described similarly in *When Hope and Fear Collide*. As with those undergraduates, student affairs staffers told stories of students coming to tell or even asking permission for a demonstration, to plan dates, times, locations, and parameters together. In one instance, a demonstration was given a 5:30 PM conclusion time by the university administration. At 5:15, it was still going strong and seemed to be picking up steam. Administrators debated what to do when the demonstrators overstayed their welcome. However, at 5:20, one of the organizers announced the demonstration was over and the students packed up and left.

However, declining interest in protest activities and campus governance should not be taken as a sign that students are uncommitted to the right of free speech or the right to demonstrate on campus. In fact, they are stronger believers in these rights than many of their predecessors. Eighty percent of undergraduates surveyed disagree with the idea that student demonstrations have no place on college campuses, a higher rate than in 1969. Seventy-five percent say college officials do not have the right to ban extreme speakers, again a higher rate than in 1969. Sixty-six percent don't think students have the right to prevent individuals with offensive views from speaking on campus, which was not part of the 1969 survey (Undergraduate Survey, 1969, 2009).

As one would expect, the issues spurring student activism today are different from those of their predecessors, not so much in kind as priority. They reflect current realities—a bad economy, wars abroad, fear of terrorism at home, a green generation, and the rise of sexual orientation as the primary diversity issue on campus. In contrast to 1993 when diversity and multiculturalism were the leading cause of student unrest, the economy is the primary issue today. At a majority of the campuses that experienced student protest in the prior year, tuition and fees were the cause. The price of textbooks, which had received scant attention from students in the previous studies, has also become a topic of concern. Fueling these issues is declining support for higher education in many states; growing numbers of students are working and working longer hours and increasing college prices at rates greater than inflation. Plus, tuition and fees are rising faster at public colleges, attended by 80 percent of undergraduates, than at private institutions.

Multicultural concerns, rooted primarily in race, have given way to issues of gay rights and sexual orientation, now the number two cause for student activism on the nation's campuses. Race has dropped to fourth in a tie with parking. Facilities, the wars, green issues, and campus safety have become more potent concerns whereas gender and free speech have diminished in importance (see Table 6.3).

Perhaps the most-telling event in recent student activism has been the Occupy Colleges protests. Intended to express solidarity with the Occupy Wall Street movement going on in cities across the United States and around the globe, Occupy Colleges

Table 6.3 Most Frequent Issues for Student Protest and Activism in the Past Year by Percent of Campuses Reporting

	1993	2009
Tuition costs and fees	37	55
Sexual orientation and gay rights	15	35
Facilities		35
Diversity and multiculturalism	48	30
Parking		30
Wars	7	20
Green issues		20
Security and safety		20
Textbook policy and prices		20
Gender	37	5
Rodney King trial	37	
Free speech	15	

Source: Campus site visits (1993, 2008).

sponsored nationwide student walkouts on campus in October and a teach-in in November 2011. A flier for the October 5, 2011, walkout is shown in Figure 6.1. It highlights several important features of the protest.

First, Occupy Colleges provided a common national banner for protest rather than usual practice of protest being local and unique to a particular campus. Whereas statewide activism, such as marches on the statehouse to protest budget cuts or tuition price increases, has been common, national protests have been rare. Only two stand out since the mid-1980s—one in opposition to South African apartheid and the other to end sweatshop labor practices.

Figure 6.1   Occupy Colleges Flier for Student Walkout, October 5, 2011
Source: Anonymous student.

Second, Occupy Colleges departed from traditional protest causes. It was not about a discreet event or activity—a war, abortion, immigration, or minority group rights—as is the norm. Instead it focused on the rather abstract issue of social class, which is currently bubbling on college campuses. The flier says, "You are the 99 percent." Occupy Colleges was about redistribution of national resources that were seen as unfairly and inequitably divided with the top 1 percent of Americans owning a disproportionate and growing share of the nation's wealth. Wall Street was seen as the epicenter of the problem. One-hundred and fifty colleges and universities, including three site-visit institutions, participated in the walkouts and sixty-nine signed up for teach-ins. The institutions initially participating in the walkout were not the usual suspects that have been the historic breeding places for student activism. None of the Ivy League universities and only a couple of the highly selective private liberal arts colleges signed on initially. Harvard, for example, was a latecomer. The list instead was dotted with community colleges, regional universities, and several of the public flagship universities. With the exception of the flagships, this is the group of campuses more likely to enroll the 99 percent. The walkout may have been historically unique for being populated by students in the mass rather than elite sector of higher education. More elite institutions signed up for the safer teach-in that followed the walkout.

Third, Occupy Colleges was a twenty-first-century protest. Although the walkout was the publicly visible element, the flier makes clear that the backbone is digital—the OccupyColleges .org website, Facebook, Twitter, and a cornucopia of other social media sites. Under the heading "WHAT CAN I DO TO HELP?" step one is start a Facebook page for your college and step six is participate in the protest.

Fourth, student support and participation was low. A 2011 study by the Harvard University Institute on Politics asked four-year college students about the Occupy Wall Street demonstrations. Thirty-nine percent of the students said they were following the demonstrations very (8 percent) or somewhat (31 percent) closely. However, only 24 percent said they were supporters; 1 percent said they had participated, 17 percent knew someone who had participated, and 16 percent thought it would have an effect on US economic policy (Institute of Politics, 2011).

The bottom line is that the Occupy Colleges protest may or may not give clues regarding the future causes and character of student protest. As to cause, Occupy Colleges and Wall Street reinforces the importance of college cost and loan indebtedness to students and it may be a harbinger of the growing importance of social class as a protest issue. As to character, it demonstrates two things we already know, which are that digital technology and social media are the life blood of student protest and participation rates have been low. However, it should be noted that participation rates in the earliest Vietnam protests were also small.

There are at least three question marks. First, Occupy Colleges and Wall Street revived two elements of past student unrest—the highly publicized mass demonstration and a common national issue. It is not clear whether these tactics have been successful or not in the minds of college students and whether they will as a result be repeated or relegated to the "we already tried that" pile. A second question mark is whether student activism will continue. If it does, will it be campus based or become more national in scope? The third question mark is whether the leadership of less selective institutions in Occupy Wall Street and Occupy Colleges is a signal of what is to come or simply an anomaly. In part, this may depend on the focus of protests. If protest is campus based, the traditionally elite institutions, which have the greatest discrepancies between their wealthiest and poorest students, may lead. If it is national, emphasizing issues such as financial aid and tuition pricing, then students at community colleges and regional universities will be the populations most affected.

Politics Beyond the Campus

Most of today's college students have lived through congressional gridlock and four embattled presidencies—Bush, Clinton, Bush, and Obama—in a nation deeply divided over religion, economics, social mores, civil liberties, and the role and scale of government. They believe meaningful social change cannot be achieved through traditional American politics (83 percent) (Undergraduate Survey, 2009).

Attitudes About Change

Undergraduates believe government is deeply troubled. In December 2011, 50 percent of college student surveyed by Harvard Institute of Politics said they disapproved of President Obama's performance; 66 percent disapproved of the performance of the Democrats in Congress; and 71 percent disapproved of the Congressional Republicans. Fifty-five percent thought the country was heading in the wrong direction (Institute of Politics, 2011).

Undergraduates also think all of our social institutions are broken—business, the courts, the family, the media, and health care. They believe corporations are too concerned with profits and not enough with public responsibilities (80 percent) and that most corporate chief executives do not deserve the high salaries they receive (72 percent). They think the courts are too concerned with the rights of criminals (51 percent). They think family values are breaking down in America (80 percent). They believe newspaper and television journalists provide biased accounts of the news (82 percent). They think doctors are motivated more by earning money than helping others (64 percent). And they believe Americans are not doing enough to bring about social changes in our society (82 percent) (Undergraduate Survey, 2009).

The political agenda for this generation is change. Students told us again and again. "We really want change." "Things need to change." "When I am older . . . I want to effect change." "You can change the future of the country." "Our generation is really going to change things." "We are going to get our education, then we will try to change the world." Undergraduates believe that one person can bring about changes in our society (62 percent) (Undergraduate Survey, 2009).

College students voted overwhelmingly for President Obama because they wanted the "change you can believe in" that he promised as a candidate. By early 2010, 46 percent of eighteen to twenty-nine-year-olds concluded things had changed in Washington, DC, and 48 percent said they hadn't. Of this age group, 56 percent attributed the lack of change to the president's opponents and special interests whereas 30 percent blamed President Obama (Pew Research Center, 2010). By 2011, Harvard Institute on Politics found more college students disapproved than approved of the president's handing of health care (55 percent), the federal budget deficit (68 percent), the economy (64 percent), and immigration (58 percent). Only on international issues did the positives equal or exceed the negatives (Institute of Politics, 2011).

Politically Disengaged

Despite their passion for change and unhappiness with the current state of the country, beyond voting, today's college students are politically disengaged from traditional politics. At the close of 2011, almost seven out of ten college students (68 percent) surveyed said they were not politically active or engaged. Even if there were a campaign they supported, fewer than half would choose to get involved in any fashion—by spreading the campaign's message to family and friends (the tribe) (43 percent), joining a Facebook group (39 percent), displaying a sticker or sign on their car or door (39 percent), attending a rally (38 percent), wearing a bracelet from the campaign (29 percent), volunteering for the campaign (25 percent), following on Twitter (20 percent),

donating money on the campaign's website (16 percent), starting
a campus group supporting the candidate (14 percent), donating
$9.99 or less on your cell phone to the campaign (13 percent), or
downloading a ringtone (9 percent) (Institute of Politics, 2011).

Issue Oriented

Since 2008, there has been a major shift in party identification
among young people. Democratic membership has plummeted,
Republican membership has grown, and Independent membership has soared. At the height of the presidential election in 2008,
the eighteen- to twenty-nine-year-old population overwhelmingly
favored the Democratic Party, more than any other age group.
Sixty-two percent labeled themselves Democrats versus 30 percent
who said they were Republicans. By 2009, the gap had closed to
49 percent Democrats and 42 percent Republicans (Pew Research
Center, 2010). In December 2011, according to the Harvard
Institute of Politics, 33 percent of college students classified themselves as Democrats, 30 percent as Republicans, and at 37 percent
Independents led the pack (Institute of Politics, 2011).

Despite their party identification in this age of gridlock politics, today's students for the most part do not see the changes that
are necessary through partisan lenses. Their political attitudes are
largely nonideological. Although a quarter of college students (24
percent) see their campuses as dominated by conservative ideology
and nearly half (44 percent) feel their campuses are dominated
by liberal ideology, the politics of today's college students defies
traditional notions of liberal and conservative (see Table 6.4)
(Undergraduate Survey, 2009).

On litmus test ideological issues, undergraduates flout ortho-
doxy. A majority of students who define themselves as liberals
oppose the abolition of capital punishment (53) and a majority of
conservatives favor handgun control (60 percent) (Undergraduate
Survey, 2009).

Table 6.4   Student Attitudes on Issues by Political Orientation
(by Percent)

	Liberal	Conservative
Capital punishment should be abolished.	47	17
Laws should be enacted to better control handgun sales and ownership.	82	60
A woman should have the freedom to choose whether or not to have an abortion.	87	40
I support homosexual and gay dating and marriage and civil unions.	85	43
Affirmative action is no longer necessary.	40	51
The US government should open more land and offshore areas for oil drilling and exploration.	40	67
Most people in poverty could do something about their situation if they really wanted to.	49	83
Illegal and undocumented immigrants should be deported.	47	79
I support raising taxes to reduce the federal deficit.	42	24
Politicians are quick to raise taxes to solve social problems.	48	75

Source: Undergraduate Survey (2009).

Sizable numbers of conservatives support liberal positions and large numbers of liberals have conservative attitudes regarding hardcore ideological issues. More than two out of five conservatives support a woman's freedom to choose to have an abortion (47 percent), gay marriage or civil unions (43 percent), and affirmative action (49 percent). Comparable numbers of liberals believe the government should open more offshore areas for oil drilling (40 percent), most people in poverty could do something about their situation if they really wanted to (49 percent), and illegal undocumented immigrants should be deported (47 percent) (Undergraduate Survey, 2009). The decline of ideology was also reported in *When Hope and Fear Collide*.

Instead today's students are issue oriented. Two of their biggest concerns, regardless of professed ideology, are the environment and the globe, which, of course, overlap.

Think Environmentally

One campus we visited was described as "so green, it's like St. Patrick's Day here." This is a green generation and whether or not that translates into environmental activism on a campus, the students we interviewed were more environmentally conscious than in the past. At least, they spoke about environmental issues much more frequently.

This is not surprising because they were born into a world that was more environmentally conscious than previous student generations. By the time the class of 2015 was born, Earth Day had been around for nearly a quarter of a century. The Oregon container recycling law, the first in the nation, had been on books for twenty years. Over a decade and a half before they were born, President Carter defined energy as one of the greatest challenges facing the nation and it has remained on the national agenda ever since. There had been environmental disasters—an oil spill in Alaska's Prince William Sound; a chemical poisoning in Bhopal, India; and nuclear accidents in Chernobyl, Russia, and Three Mile Island, Pennsylvania. The term *global warming* was already in use, too.

While they grew up, the environment gained priority as an issue, fueled by a steady tattoo of events—the Kyoto Protocol on Climate when they were four years old, Hurricane Katrina when they were twelve, the film *An Inconvenient Truth* on the dangers of global warming when they were thirteen, Al Gore winning the

Nobel Peace Prize for his work on climate change when they were fourteen, the BP oil spill when they were seventeen, and the devastating earthquakes in Haiti and Japan when they seventeen and eighteen years old.

It's no wonder that environmentalism and sustainability, the generational responsibility to manage the use of resources for the future, which has become very widely embraced at least rhetorically in the twenty-first century, is a sprawling enterprise in higher education. There are national, regional, and local organizations for students, faculty members, administrators, and whole campuses. They deal with the environment and sustainability broadly or focus on specific aspects of it—food, water, transportation, energy, green buildings, recycling, investment policy, and so much more. They offer an assortment of services including research, report cards, best practices, career counseling, training for activists, resource centers, speakers, conferences, webinars, events, networking, and on and on. There are environmental organizations for different ethnic, religious, gender, sexual and political orientations, geographic locales, and just about any other distinction that can be found among people.

Environment is a staple in college and university academic offerings. In 1965, Middlebury College established the first environmental studies program. Today there are more than a thousand.

It's a part of student life. More than two out of three four-year colleges (69 percent) and one in six two-year colleges have environmental awareness or preservation groups (Student Affairs Survey, 2008). Typical of most of campus groups we encountered is the Vassar College Greens, which describes itself this way:

> The Vassar Greens are an environmental activist group with projects ranging from on campus, local and regional initiatives. The 50–60 member group meets as a general

body on Wednesday nights at 8 pm in the Jade Parlor, and meets as smaller, focused campaign groups during other evenings. The campaigns focus on initiatives such as shutting down a local incinerator, running the Free Market, putting composting in the dorms, shifting Vassar's energy usage away from coal power, and kicking bottled water off campus (Main Circle, 2010).

In the final analysis, despite the powerful network of organizations and activities knit together in varying degree by websites, Facebook pages, Twitter feeds, and blogs, environmental and sustainability activities boil down to the individual campus. Activism in this area is local. It's about the Vassar Greens and their leaders at colleges and universities across the country. The effectiveness of these organizations waxes and wanes annually with the quality of their leaders.

However, the continuing power and efficacy of environmentalism on campus remains and can be attributed to several factors. First, today's students have embraced it. Though this is a fiscally conservative generation who oppose raising taxes to reduce the deficit (65percent) and think politicians are too quick to raise taxes to support social programs (62 percent), they would support greater government spending to address energy sufficiency and global warming (76 percent) and would be willing to pay more taxes to support energy conservation and protect the environment (63 percent). However, they are not purists. At best they are pragmatic and at worst inconsistent in their environmental beliefs. They want energy independence and are willing to employ methods for accomplishing it that have not been thought of as environmentally friendly such as expanding the use of nuclear energy (57 percent) and opening up more land and offshore areas for oil drilling and exploration (54 percent) (Undergraduate Survey, 2009).

Nonetheless, the fact that this is a green generation is reflected in students being interested and receptive to environmental appeals

but it does not turn them into activists or even members of organizations like the Vassar Greens. For those who do become activists, there are training events. For example, students at Yale held
a one-day leadership conference for New England and Middle
Atlantic college environmental activists, which we learned about
on Facebook and the CampusActivism.org website. It offered
workshops on organizing, recruiting, outreach, and campus actions
from campus activists; networking opportunities to share the lessons of campus-led initiatives; panels on how to work with the
administration; and updates on current national and regional campaigns as well as organic food and an environmental fair.

Second, events such as the gas price hike and Hurricane
Katrina, which were high on student lists of key events in their
lives, have served to spark action on issues such as energy sufficiency and environment. With regard to Katrina, students and
college administrators on most campuses believed it spiked environmental consciousness and encouraged community service, but
the effect was short term. We visited many campuses from Alaska
to Florida, from California to Connecticut, where students went
on service missions to New Orleans in the months and weeks after
the hurricane, but at most schools' interest trailed off within a
year and dissipated after a second year. The editor of a midwestern
research university newspaper said, "It's almost like you are supposed to care at this time, so let's care . . . for six months and then
they kind of move on." Deans and students alike said the lasting
effect of Katrina was disillusionment with government.

Third, for administrators and faculty members, environmentalism has also become a more pressing concern. This has been
driven by laws in areas such as recycling and emissions, the rising
cost of energy in university budgets, student pressure, growing
environmental consciousness on the part of adults, and a belief by
many campus staff that it's the right thing to do.

As a result, it was rare to visit a campus—two year or four year
in any region of the country—and not hear about environmental

activism or have administrators point with pride to green buildings or plans to make use of an alternative energy source such
as wind or solar power or the purchase of hybrid cars for the
security force.

Talk Globally

More than ever before, students who grew up in a flattening world
with weaker nation states described themselves as members of a
global society rather than simply Americans. Our generation lives
under "more of a global banner," we were told. Indeed, when students talked about issues ranging from the environment, energy,
and civil liberties to the economy, jobs, and their physical safety,
they often spoke of them in an international context.

Large numbers of undergraduates have had international
experience. Almost three out of five students (59 percent) at four-
year colleges and a third at community colleges (34 percent) have
lived, studied, or traveled abroad and a majority (54 percent)
believe undergraduate education would be improved if students
were required to spend a year abroad (Undergraduate Survey,
2009). Many are doing that. More than a million students in each
college-entering class will study abroad before earning their baccalaureate degree (Institute on International Education, 2010).

Students today are more interested in international than
domestic issues. Eighty-two percent of the undergraduates surveyed said they are very interested in global issues and concerns in
contrast to 52 percent who expressed interest in national politics
(Undergraduate Survey, 2009). But the globalism of today's students doesn't match traditional notions of international engagement. A majority of current undergraduates are international
isolationists, meaning they would have the United States less
involved with the rest of the world. They believe the United States
government should focus more on its own problems than on those
of other countries (58 percent) and the problems of other nations

cannot be solved by outside assistance (64 percent). They reject the notion that the US government is not doing enough to help solve problems in other countries (62 percent). They think Iraq and North Korea should be allowed to develop nuclear technology if they wish (63 percent) (Undergraduate Survey, 2009).

Their view of immigration is also restrictive. Although only a minority approve of government plans to build a fence or wall along the US border to control illegal immigration (42 percent), most believe illegal and undocumented immigrants should be deported (60 percent), denied in-state tuition rates (70 percent), and be barred from participating in federal and state financial aid programs (74 percent). Undergraduates overwhelmingly oppose granting illegal immigrants amnesty (70 percent), though a small majority do support guest worker visas (55 percent) (Undergraduate Survey, 2009).

In addition, today's students don't know very much about the world, as shown in Table 6.5. As mentioned previously, they do not recognize the names of the world leaders whose actions are covered daily in the media and whose nations for ill or for good

Table 6.5 Names Unrecognized by Undergraduates (by Percent)

Hu Jin Tau, president of China	80
Henry Paulsen, US secretary of treasury at time of survey	74
Robert Mugabe, president of Zimbabwe	72
Nicolas Sarkozy, president of France at time of survey	69
John Roberts, chief justice, US Supreme Court	66
David Patraeus, currently director of the CIA, formerly US army general at time of survey	65
Mahmoud Amadinejad, president of Iran	60
Joseph McCarthy, former US senator	60

(Continued)

Table 6.5 *(continued)*

Michael Bloomberg, mayor of New York City and communications entrepreneur	57
Kim Jong Il, supreme leader of North Korea	51
Mikhail Gorbachev, former president of the Soviet Union	50
Sandra Day O'Connor, first woman justice on US Supreme Court	44
Nancy Pelosi, speaker of the US House of Representatives at the time of the survey	37
Rush Limbaugh, talk show host	36
Nelson Mandela, former president of South Africa	27
Ralph Nader, consumer advocate and former presidential candidate	23
Ted Kennedy, US senator at the time of the survey	21
Jesse Jackson, former presidential candidate and civil rights activist	17
Joseph Biden, vice president of the United States	16
Condeleeza Rice, former US secretary of state	11
Miley Cyrus, performer	9
Fidel Castro, former president of Cuba	9
Ronald Reagan, former US president	5
Tiger Woods, athlete	2

Source: Undergraduate Survey (2009).

are shaping the future of the globe. Their ignorance extends to the leaders of their own country.

Current undergraduates have a very different view of globalism. It is at once personal, meaning they see their generation as composed not only of young people in the United States, but also of peers from around the world. They are far more interested in the digital natives who protested in the Arab Spring via Twitter and Facebook and believe they have more in common with them than the heads of state who lead their countries.

For undergraduates, their brand of globalism is also issue oriented and transcends national borders. Whether pollution occurs in China or the United States is irrelevant. It's still pollution. In focus group interviews, students told us their generation would "save the dolphin," find solutions to "global warming," and create a more "equitable global economy." These are worldwide issues. The remedies won't be found in a single country. When undergraduates spoke to us of their generation, they were often talking about a global generation.

News Sources

Students get their news in different ways than their predecessors. As might be expected, their primary source is the Internet (78 percent). Following are television (75 percent), print media (50 percent), other people (44 percent), and radio (40 percent) (Undergraduate Survey, 2009). When asked what they meant by "other people," they spoke of one historic form of communication—chitchat—and they mentioned a twenty-first century approach: news stories sent by their tribe via e-mail or websites recommended by friends and others whose opinions they value.

Young people today have an absolutely astounding array of choices for getting news—every website in cyberspace, thousands of radio and television stations, and an enormous assortment of print media. The consequence is that there is no common source of news content or even what could be called common content. The common sources of content of the past have largely disappeared. The daily newspaper and network news shows are in decline. Today there is no Walter Cronkite, the 1960s and 1970s CBS news anchorman often referred to as "the most trusted man in America."

When undergraduates were asked which news source they preferred, their top choices were CNN (31 percent), *New York Times* (12 percent), Fox (8 percent), MSNBC (6 percent), local newspapers (6 percent), BBC (4 percent), ABC (3 percent), the *Daily Show* (2 percent), and Yahoo! (2 percent). No other source was named by more than 1 percent of undergraduates (Undergraduate Survey, 2009). In short, there is no news source read, listened to, or watched by a majority of undergraduates.

So it is unlikely, even unrealistic to expect, that people have a common body of knowledge regarding world affairs or most other subjects. Not only has media content exploded, but so have the number of devices for receiving content. This combination has shifted media from a shared cultural experience to an individual phenomenon. There is no longer a need for the entire family to sit together in the living room watching the same television show broadcast by one of the three national networks on the one TV in their home and then talking about it the next day with their fellow students, coworkers, and neighbors who had seen the show as well. Today, each person constructs his or her own media diet, perhaps with aid from the members of his or her tribe. If a person wants to avoid the news, she can. If a person wants news, he has a seemingly endless array of options. The news can be presented from a liberal or conservative perspective or from the point of view of a specific race, religion, nationality, or ethnicity. It can be local, regional, national, or international. The focus of the news can be a particular subject—sports, finance, or entertainment. Reality TV can be the war in Afghanistan or *American Idol*. Given the people current college students know and don't know, the latter appears the more popular choice for undergraduates.

There is a news program on National Public Radio called "All Things Considered." In this era when difference seems to trump commonality in media, a series of programs called "A Few Things

Considered" or perhaps "One Thing Considered" might be more attractive to college students.

Act Locally

As with their heroes, activism on the part of students is local and most often takes the form of service. One dean described the situation this way: "Students are increasingly concerned and involved with local issues that affect them and with service to the community. I believe we have seen an increased commitment from students to help solve local problems . . . I believe students are increasingly caring about the welfare of others (Student Affairs Survey, 2011).

Undergraduates say they are focusing locally because they don't feel they have the power or ability to deal with global issues such as climate change, but they can address them in their neighborhood or community by working on remedies such as recycling, staffing a green market, or helping to build more energy-efficient homes. Direct services, such as tutoring, cleaning the local pond, and helping out at a soup kitchen, all make a concrete difference in people's lives. These activities are real and they are tangible, which is essential to a pragmatic generation, not Don Quixote–like in their attitudes or actions. For a protected generation, it is not surprising that current undergraduates are more partial to white collar voluntarism than getting their hands dirty. Fundraising, tutoring, and advocacy have greater appeal than hospice, relief, and homelessness work. As young people, they gravitate more toward children than seniors. All of this was true of the students of the 1990s as well.

Two out of three students (65 percent) report that they were engaged in service activities during the past twelve months, more at four-year schools (81 percent) than community colleges (48 percent). This was true in the last survey as well. No matter how one slices and dices the student population, a majority are involved in service—Asian Americans (54 percent), blacks (64 percent), Hispanics (58 percent), whites (68 percent), men (61 percent), women (68 percent), students under twenty-four years old (66 percent), students over twenty-four (60 percent), freshmen (81 percent), seniors (55 percent), part-time attendees (52 percent), full-timers (68 percent), students working ten or fewer hours a week (77 percent), student working eleven to twenty hours per week (71 percent), students working twenty-one to thirty-five hours a week (66 percent), and students working more than thirty-six hours or more a week (51 percent) (Undergraduate Survey, 1993, 2009). The pattern closely mirrors participation rates in out-of-class activities on campus, discussed in Chapter Three.

These students are involved in a cornucopia of different activities, ranging from hospices and pet protection to homelessness and choice and right to life groups, as shown in Table 6.6.

The three most popular have remained constant since the last survey—church and religious activities, work for charity organizations such as the United Way, and child and youth work. Church and religious activities have become the most popular, increasing from the choice of a quarter (24 percent) to a third of all students (32 percent) (Undergraduate Survey, 1993, 2009). This is consistent with the fact that nearly half of the campuses surveyed (48 percent) reported increases in student participation in spiritual and faith-based groups since 2001, again more frequently at four-year colleges (58 percent) than at two-year schools (32 percent) (Student Affairs Survey, 2008).

However, this is not to say that students have become more religious or that religion has become a more important aspect of their lives. As in the last survey, about a quarter of college students (23 percent) described themselves as fundamentalists. Most undergraduates label themselves moderately religious (52 percent), but three times as many say they are opposed to or indifferent to

Table 6.6   Percent of Students Participating in Most Popular Service Activities (Involving 10 Percent or More of Students Engaged in Service Activities) by Institutional Type

Service Activity	Two year	Four year	Total
Church or religion related programs	25	39	32
Child and youth organizations	13	36	25
Charity organizations (e.g., United Way)	15	35	24
Cancer	12	28	20
Neighborhood or community clean-up programs	11	25	18
Elderly and senior citizens	14	20	17
Alcohol and drugs	9	18	14
Homelessness and housing (e.g., Habitat for Humanity)	7	19	13
Education and arts organizations (e.g., zoos, museums, libraries, and theaters)	6	20	13
Hospital, health care, hospice	9	16	12
Environment	8	17	12
Election campaigns	7	18	12
Domestic hunger, human relief, development	7	16	12
Animal protection	6	15	11
Women	8	12	10
Election reform, voter registration	7	12	10
Learning disabilities	5	13	9
Abortion and family planning (pro and con)	7	9	8
Mental health	5	8	7
Physical disabilities	7	8	7

(Continued)

Table 6.6 *(continued)*

Service Activity	Two year	Four year	Total
Civil rights	4	10	7
AIDS	4	10	7
International hunger, human relief, development	3	10	7
Domestic violence	6	8	7
Human rights (international and domestic)	4	9	6
Hispanic American	3	8	6
Blind, deaf, and hearing impaired	2	8	5
African American	3	6	5
Gun control pro or con	5	3	4
Veterans, military support, and advocacy	2	6	4
Immigration reform and control	1	4	3
Native American	1	4	3
Peace and international relations	2	5	3
Public interest research groups (PIRGS)	2	4	3
Asian American		5	2

Source: Undergraduate Survey (2009).

religion (37 percent) as deeply religious (11 percent). They are also twice as likely never or rarely to attend religious services (59 percent) as to go at least weekly (28 percent). For most undergraduates, their religious attitudes have not changed in college either. A large majority consider themselves as religious now as before they started college (68 percent), but slightly more say they are less (19 percent) than more religious (14 percent) (Undergraduate Survey, 2009). With the exception of the sectarian colleges we visited, religion was not a topic that surfaced often in our conversations with student affairs staffers or undergraduates, despite interviewer's probes.

Among the least popular of the service activities were those that were explicitly international or dealt with race and ethnic issues, which makes sense given the local nature of service for students, the fact that undergraduates talk more than act globally, and that race and ethnic concerns are less heated on campus.

The reasons students participate in service activities are just about as varied as the activities. The rationales were frequently instrumental. A fifth (22 percent) of the participants said they were volunteered. That is, they were required to be altruistic for a class, a social group, to graduate, to fulfill financial aid requirements, or the like. Some were quite candid in saying service would "look good on my résumé or teach me skills that might be useful in the job market." It was also considered an excellent meat market by a number, a good way to meet potential dating partners. A few said they stumbled into it. There are now a number of organizations nationally that promote college student service such as Project Prometheus, Campus Compact, and Alternative Spring Break. Students told us of having seen a flier or run into a website advertising a service experience, especially Alternative Spring Break, which offers students the opportunity to spend a week doing community service rather than vacationing during the week designated for spring break on their campus. A couple of students said they signed up because it was a lot better than going home.

But most often, students said they participated because "I want to make a difference." This is a generation that almost universally says it is important to them to do good and help people (97 percent). Service is also a way to produce the change that is so important to them. Students said service gave them "hope," a feeling of making a "contribution," "good feelings" about myself, a sense of "doing something to help," and "satisfaction."

Their commitment is not large—a median and mode of eleven to twenty hours a year. The average is 30.4 hours, about an hour a week per semester. It is down slightly from the 1990s when the mean was 36.4 hours. In fact, although the proportion of student participating in service has increased significantly compared to the 1970s and 1980s, the amount of time undergraduates are spending on service has decreased. A major cause is the economy. As indicated previously, the more hours students work, the lower their participation in service. In 2009, 72 percent of Americans said they cut back on civic engagement owing to the recession (Main Circle, 2010).

Most students would be like to do more service if there were compensation of sorts. They would be willing to spend a year or two in community service (55 percent) or teaching (54 percent) after graduation for a reduction in college costs, which should not be seen as mercenary. It would be a trade-off for the work they are doing to pay their tuition and living expenses now. In interviews, students often said they would prefer service assignments over their current jobs, even at lower rates of pay. However, the proportion of students who make the trade drops when the community service is teaching in urban or low-income schools (45 percent) or military service (12 percent). Fewer than two in five of the students surveyed (38 percent) think undergraduate education would be improved if students were required to spend a year in community service (Undergraduate Survey; 2009).

The inescapable conclusion is that today's college students are engaged to an even larger degree than many of their predecessors. They are acting more individually and less visibly. They have not locked themselves in their rooms to play video games, nor has the economy driven them away from helping others. This generation is quietly engaged, outside traditional social institutions and politics. The causes that have the most potential power to raise the noise level are financial, related to college costs, and loan obligations.

7

The Future

CLINGING TO THE AMERICAN DREAM

Students continue to be optimistic and hopeful . . .
—SENIOR STUDENT AFFAIRS OFFICER, WESTERN RESEARCH UNIVERSITY

Students are not as hopeful about the future.
—SENIOR STUDENT AFFAIRS OFFICER, MIDWESTERN
REGIONAL UNIVERSITY

THIS IS a generation that grew up in boom times and attended college during a bust. They saw soaring unemployment rates and plunging real estate values, accompanied by landmark foreclosures. They witnessed a stock market crash and rebound with yo-yo-like daily fluctuations. They observed as major nations—Greece, Iceland, Ireland, Italy, Portugal, and Spain—teetered at the edge of default and the future of the European Union stood in the balance. They watched as China rose in world prominence and the United States appeared to be receding. They lived through a recession that seemed never to end with a government gridlocked and unable to act and public trust and hope eroding.

Today's students are graduating from college to enter a job market in which 9.1 percent of recent grads are unemployed. Two-thirds are leaving not only with a diploma, but also with student loan debts averaging $31,050 for a baccalaureate degree (Lewin, 2011). And one in four eighteen- to twenty-nine-year-olds, previously living on his or her own, is moving back with his or her parents (Pew Social Trends Center, 2010). As noted in Chapter One, for many the recession determined which college they attended, what they studied, how many courses they could take, and where they lived. This situation was highlighted in many of the signs and postings at the Occupy Wall Street demonstrations—"I have $50,000 in student loan debt and my BA is useless"; "graduated from college May 2010; debt: $35,000; jobs in US: none"; and "I have always believed in the American Dream, but the 1 percent stole that" (*We are the 99 percent*, 2011; Occupy Wall Street signs and postings; Nelson, 2011). Student affairs staff describe current college students as "anxious," "frustrated," and most often "stressed" (Student Affairs Survey, 2011).

In spite of all of this, this is a generation with higher personal and material aspirations than their predecessors. They are counting on the American Dream being available to them as it was for past generations of college students. Current undergraduates want good jobs and are willing to forego their careers of choice to get them. For instance, 23 percent of the students surveyed plan on business careers, but only 7 percent say it is the career they are most interested in. The same is true of medicine and health. Seventeen percent expect to enter those fields, but only 8 percent prefer them. The reverse is the case with the arts, a field in which 6 percent plan to work, but 11 percent would like to. Similarly, less than 1 percent of students are planning on careers as homemakers, but 4 percent would choose to (Undergraduate Survey, 2009).

They want successful relationships. Eighty-nine percent say it's important to have a good marriage or relationship, which is 3 percentage points less than in 1993 (Undergraduate Survey, 2009).

They want to have children (89 percent). This is 11 percentage points higher than in 1993 and 15 percentage points more than in 1976 (Undergraduate Survey, 1976, 1993, 2009).

They want money and material goods. Eighty-three percent of the students surveyed said its very important to them to become very well off financially, which is 8 percentage points higher than in 1993 and 20 percentage points more than in 1976 (Undergraduate Surveys, 1976, 1993, 2009).

They expect to be at least as well off as their parents (73 percent), a percentage point more than in 1993 (Undergraduate Survey, 1976, 1993, 2009). They say this even though 79 percent are concerned that Social Security will not be able to provide the benefits they expect when they retire (Institute of Politics, 2011).

This generation holds contradictory views of the world in which they hope to accomplish all of these things. It is, on the one hand, a Hobbesian place where each wars against all. College students believe most people only look out for themselves (77 percent) and will take advantage of you if they can (69 percent). They think life isn't fair—economic well-being in the United States is unjustly and unfairly distributed (66 percent) (Undergraduate Survey, 2009).

On the other hand, they are latter-day Horatio Algers, believing as did the nineteenth-century novelist that with hard work, determination, and character anyone can succeed in America, rising even from poverty to great wealth. Today's undergraduates believe that hard work always pays off (83 percent), if you want something you should have to work to earn it (97 percent), most people who live in poverty could do something about their condition (67 percent), and everyone has the ability to complete a college education if only they could afford to attend (68 percent) (Undergraduate Survey, 2009).

The combination evokes the image of the Lone Ranger, pure of heart, determined, and industrious, outnumbered in a hostile landscape, yet triumphant week after week after week. This, of course, seems a bit incongruous with the notion of a student asking his mom to call the dean to complain about his roommate. (But to be completely candid, the reader should know that Diane was too young to have watched the *Lone Ranger* on television and Arthur did not see every show, so there may indeed have been an episode in which at the Lone Ranger's behest, his mother called the sheriff to demand justice for her wronged son. Were there "bronco" or "barbed-wire" parents?)

In any case, this sense of "rugged individualism," compartmentalization, or magical thinking is reflected in student optimism about the future. Nine out of ten undergraduates surveyed (89 percent) were optimistic about their personal futures, 1 percentage point higher than in 1993, but only slightly more than a third (35 percent) were optimistic about the country's future, a question that was not included in the 1993 survey. When asked to choose a number from one to ten, with one being lowest and ten being highest, to describe their level of optimism regarding themselves and the nation, students assigned an average of 7.7 to themselves and 4.8 to the country (Undergraduate Survey, 2009).

We asked them why they were pessimistic about the future of the country. Students cited a litany of problems facing the United States and the world. It was the raft of issues, which have been discussed in previous chapters, ranging from social, economic, and global troubles to the inequity and unfairness of the distribution of power and resources, the inability or unwillingness of government to act, and a general sense of national decline. Here's a sampling of what they told us and the issues they raised:

- The United States "lost a ton of respect in the global community."
- "We will be a third-world country."
- "Globalization," "multinational corporations," "industry going abroad"
- "Energy," "oil dependence"
- "Conflict with Islamic world"
- "Wars, leaderships hiding the truth from us, millions of dollars required to run for president"; "it's all about money"
- "Natural disasters such as Hurricane Katrina"; "lack of action after Hurricane Katrina"
- "Environment and the quality of education"
- "All the lobbying, but rarely for public interest; they [government] are more for industry."
- "Government gridlock"
- "Politicians are more worried about getting elected than serving their constituents."
- There is "a widening gap between the lowest socioeconomic group and the highest."
- "Health care," "high uninsured"
- "Social Security"
- "Debt," "economy"
- "Unemployment"
- "World hunger"
- "Slave labor"
- "Biased news"
- "Big Brother"
- "Society is going downhill rapidly."

- "We're getting more selfish, more materialistic, and obese."
- "Our time is dwindling."

The comments of student focus group interviews regarding the state of the nation and world were overwhelmingly negative. These conversations gave the sense that undergraduates were passengers on the *Titanic*.

So we asked students, given all of the negatives, the long list of problems, the breadth of the problems, and the sense of deteriorating conditions, how they could possibly be optimistic about their personal futures. After all, two-thirds of them will graduate with large student loan debts; one in eleven will be unemployed; and one in four will have to go back to living with his or her parents. Their answer was basically that "I am not going to be one of the statistics. I will beat the odds. I have a big future ahead and the support to achieve it." Bear in mind that more than 10 percent were not optimistic about their futures and others thought they would have to overcome major obstacles to succeed and were worried or at least concerned about what they were facing. However, these are the rationales students gave for being optimistic:

- "I don't have dreams of making a ton of money. I have very basic desires in my life. I am about to marry a kickass girl. I am very fortunate to have wonderful friends and I am going into a field I am passionate about, so I am feeling pretty good about myself."
- "I am attending one of the most prestigious colleges in America."
- "I have been surrounded by enough people in my life who had enough confidence in me. I feel like I will be personally successful in whatever I do."
- "I already have a job with McKinsey [a prestigious international consulting firm]."

- "I have a great supportive family and I have a firm belief in Christ . . . and also the field I am going into has lots of job listings, physical therapy."

- "I know where I want to go and what I want to do."

- "My parents provided me with the resources to be successful"; "[I have a] really supportive family."

- "I just figure I am going to get a job, house, family. I feel I will be comfortable."

- "I will 'shoot for the moon' and land among the stars."

- "I have the support I need, the will, and drive."

- "The university has given me so much as far as maturity and confidence."

- "I'm pretty sure I can play in the game, so I'm pretty optimistic."

Most of the students we interviewed mentioned family support as an important element in why they thought they would succeed. In fact, over two-thirds noted family and friends as the key to their optimism. In many ways, the student optimism was rooted in the factors that have been discussed throughout this book—the centrality of parents in undergraduates' lives and the support and continuing connection to their tribe. For ill or for good, their optimism also rested on the high self-esteem of a generation of students who have never skinned their knees and have won awards throughout their lives. The question, of course, is whether this will be an asset, enabling them to thrive in hard times, because the idea of failure is unimaginable or will be a liability, making college students less resilient for lack of experience, coping with previous wounds and giving them a misplaced sense of invulnerability.

8

Conclusion

THE FUTURE IS A FOREIGN COUNTRY

> *Now this is not the end. It is not even the beginning of the*
> *end. But it is, perhaps, the end of the beginning.*
>
> —WINSTON CHURCHILL, LORD MAYOR'S LUNCHEON,
> MANSION HOUSE, NOVEMBER 10, 1942

WHEN DREAMS *and Heroes Died* was a portrait of an
undergraduate generation growing up in a national, analog, industrial economy. When *Hope and Fear Collide* was a picture of a college generation straddling two worlds—one was the
world of their predecessors, a receding national, analog, industrial economy, and the other was an emerging global, digital, and
information economy.

This book began where the last concluded. It is a snapshot of
the first generation of college students to be born in a global, digital, information economy. This chapter discusses the nature of that
world; the ways in which it likely to flower, develop, and mature
in the years ahead; and the demands that it will make on its citizens. It contrasts those demands with the characteristics of today's
undergraduates discussed in previous chapters; the attitudes,

values, and experiences they bring to college. It finds that current students are ill prepared to face the future and the nation's colleges and universities will have to make major changes to provide students with the education they need. A proposal for how this might be accomplished is offered. This chapter also examines the challenges and opportunities this generation poses for employers, parents, and government.[1]

The Twenty-First Century

We are at the dawn of the global, digital, information economy. The current generation of college students was born into this world but relatively early in its inception. To put this into historical context, it is as if they had been born in the initial decades of the Industrial Revolution, the second of the world's three great transformations—the agricultural revolution, the industrial revolution, and the current era—which will be named by historians decades from now. Imagine the children born in 1840. They were born after what came to be called the *transportation revolution* was well underway. Canals, steamboats, and trains were realities. The first American railroad line, the Baltimore and Ohio, was created more than a decade before their birth. Agricultural machines such as the thresher, the cotton gin, and the plough had already been invented. Factories, the keystone of the Industrial Revolution, had firmly taken root and were growing quickly. Young people born in 1840 might have ridden on a train, worked in a factory, or used the new farm implements. Perhaps the time in which they were born could be characterized as the end of the beginning of the Industrial Revolution and maybe that generation of children could be described as the first industrial natives.

But during their lifetimes, if they lived to age seventy, these young people would witness the flowering of the Industrial Revolution. Railroads would crisscross the continent and America would change from a country of localities to a nation spanning two oceans, knit together not only by tracks but also by the telegraph and telephone, invented after they were born. They would see water and steam power yield to petroleum and electricity. America's population would move from the farms to the cities, giving birth to great metropolises that would soon sprout skyscrapers and later be lighted with electricity. Things as basic as the age at which people married, the size of their families, the hours they worked, where they lived and labored, and the sources of their food and clothing would change.

America would become a nation of large corporations. Early industrial giants such as Peter Cooper, an entrepreneur, train inventor, and one-time presidential candidate, would be succeeded by railroad magnates such as Jay Gould, E. H. Harriman, and Leland Stanford. Robert Fulton, the artist and steam boat pioneer, would give way to shipping magnates such as Commodore Cornelius Vanderbilt. Samuel Slater, who brought the factory to America, would be replaced by automotive tycoon Henry Ford. Steel and oil would fuel the revolution led by barons such as Andrew Carnegie and John D. Rockefeller. Bankers, epitomized by J. P. Morgan, would create the institutions necessary to finance this sprawling enterprise and enable its expansion. The race for the presidency in 1896 would be a battle between America's past as an agricultural nation and its future as an industrial power. There would be a raft of new laws, regulations, and legal decisions to govern the new economy. Colleges would become universities. Time zones would be created because commerce required it and unions would be established because labor demanded them. The train would beget cars, trucks, turbine-powered ships, motorcycles, zeppelins, and airplanes before the seventieth birthdays of the generation of 1840.

The children born in 1840 entered a world different than their parents—technologically, economically, geographically, and demographically. By the time, they were eighteen, the age of current college freshmen, that world had changed still more with the advance of industrialization. However, much that we associate with the industrial age—the oil well, oil pipeline, telephone, transcontinental railroad, mass-production steel mills, the assembly line, the lightbulb, and even the zipper—were yet to be created or make their appearance in the United States. The names that would be most closely associated with industrialization were at most young people, too. When those born in 1840 turned eighteen, Andrew Carnegie was twenty-three years old; Jay Gould was twenty-two, John D. Rockefeller was nineteen, Thomas Edison was eleven, and E. H. Harriman was ten. Of the two candidates who would wage the 1896 presidential campaign, one was fifteen years old and the other had not yet been born, nor for that matter had Henry Ford.

The industrial revolution came to fruition not before the generation of 1840 was born, not while they were growing up, but in their adulthood. It was their great-grandchildren who were born into and grew up in a fully articulated and mature industrial society.

The situation of current college students is likely to be similar to their 1840 counterparts. However, the pace of change promises to be far swifter today than in 1840 and what was a six-generation process of US industrialization, beginning with the grandparents of the generation of 1840 and concluding with their great-grandchildren, is likely to be compressed today. The point is this. Current undergraduates are living in a world in which the scale, rapidity, and profundity of change is likely to be relentless. They are the global, digital, information economy citizens 1.0 who will live their lives in a world hurtling toward 2.0 and perhaps beyond. For them, the future promises to be a different country. They will do things differently there.

Global, digital, information economy 2.0 will see the next phase of globalization. It is accepted wisdom that we live in a global society and common knowledge that it is growing flatter, more interconnected, and more mutually dependent. But we have no idea yet what a global society really is or what a flat world looks like. Is it a world much like that of the present with far closer ties among nations and between the people who live in those nations? Is it a world with more unions and alliances among nations similar to the European Union? Is it a world in which nation states have withered and the boundaries between countries have little meaning? Is it a shared world government? Is it the world portrayed in countless movies and novels, many dreadful, in which multinational corporations replace government? Is it a more democratic world or more of a big brother–type place? Are resources better or more poorly distributed? Is it a safer or more dangerous world? Will flattening breed homogeneity or provide greater opportunities for diversity? One can create an endless number of scenarios of what globalization means but the simple fact is that no one knows. What is undeniable is that current college students will live in an era of global change, which promises to be profound, and some of those students will have to help shape it.

Global, digital, information economy 2.0 will also bring new technologies as well as advances in existing technologies. We know some things that are on the horizon: nanotechnology, biotechnology, robotics, cognitive science, artificial intelligence, and infotechnology. We can name them but we do not know their consequences. Nor do we know the degree to which applications of existing technologies will cause change in the world or as-yet-unknown technologies will emerge with profound results. We don't know which technologies will be disruptive or what aspects of our lives they will disrupt. That's the realm of science fiction. What we do know is that current college students will live through an era of technological change, which promises to be profound, and some of those students will have to help to shape it.

Global, digital, information economy 2.0 will additionally see the further unfolding of the information economy. Among many things, this will require us to rethink our social institutions—government, schools, health care, media, and finance—which were created for a different time, for an industrial era. Today, they all seem to be broken, less good than they once were. That's what undergraduates told us. It's what Americans are saying to pollsters over and over again with increasing levels of cynicism and declining levels of hope. Government is in gridlock, the schools are poor in quality, health care is a mess, media is biased and not worthy of trust, and our financial institutions are avaricious and nearly destroyed the world economy. In response, the nation is simultaneously moving in two very different directions to retrofit these institutions: reform of the existing institutions undertaken from inside and outside and replacement of those institutions in the belief that they cannot be reformed. Government is the one real exception to this approach because replacement is also called treason, though this did not prove a barrier in the Arab Spring.

Think about our schools as an example. Today change is coming on three fronts. The first is internal reform in which superintendents in some school districts are making major efforts to improve their existing schools. The second front is external reform, in which initiatives such as charter schools and alternative routes to careers in teaching as well as organizations such as Teach For America, KIPP (Knowledge Is Power Program), and Mosaica are attempting to improve the existing schools from outside. Third, efforts are underway to replace the existing schools, which are seen by proponents of this approach as so mired in antiquated visions of education as to be unsalvageable. The goal here is to reinvent schools via initiatives such as online schooling, home schooling, and the creation of new schools that dispense with uniform, time-based education in favor individualized and outcome-based schooling.

In varying degree, the same thing is happening to every one of our social institutions. The changes appear to be furthest along in media, where the historic leaders—the major networks, newspapers, magazines, music companies, publishers, bookstores, and other knowledge-producing and -distributing organizations—are in serious decline. Their pricing and sales models no longer work. The neighborhood independent bookshops are all but gone and megabookstores are closing. Music stores are a relic of the past. Their businesses have moved to the Internet. New organizations have sprung up to replace them and the number of content providers has multiplied. Media has moved from a producer to a consumer-driven industry that is specialized, individualized, shared, technology-based, more convenient, cheaper, and operates 24/7. The web browser makes media public and raises the importance of the content producer over the distributor in an industry that is moving to eliminate the intermediaries between producers and consumers.

One might expect other social institutions to follow similar paths, but once again we can only guess what form a mature knowledge economy and the institutions on which it rests will take. But we do know this. Today's college students will live in an era of economic and social change, which promises to be profound, and some students will have to help to shape it.

Today's College Students

The current generation of college students is not prepared for this world. They lack many of the skills, much of the knowledge, and a good deal of the perspective it will require. On average, today's students are the following:

- Digital natives
- Weak in face-to-face social skills
- Tribal in their relationships

- Immature, needy, timid, protected, and tethered to their parents, who are their heroes
- Self-absorbed, polite, rule observers, and good with adults
- Hard hit by the recession
- Pragmatic, career oriented, and determined to do well
- Hard working, but confuse the quantity of work they do with the quality of the product
- Consumer oriented and entitled
- Optimistic about their personal futures
- Pessimistic about the future of the country
- Demanding of change
- Disenchanted with politics and the nation's social institutions
- Issue oriented rather than ideological
- Global talkers, green thinkers, and local actors
- Engaged in service and wanting to do good
- Little involved in campus life
- Sexually active but interpersonally awkward
- Abusers of alcohol and heavy users of psychological counseling services
- Weak in basic skills and cultural knowledge
- Lacking in decorum related to technology and understanding of academic rules and values
- More comfortable with racial, ethnic, and gender differences
- Desperately committed to American Dream

Today's college students have real strengths, which are unique to this generation, with regard to the future that awaits them. They are digital natives in what will be a flowering of the digital age, they are more comfortable with diversity than the previous student generations in a society growing more multicultural, they think globally in a flattening world, they are experienced networkers in an age in which boundaries are breaking and team work is growing more and more important, and they are experienced with and demanding of change in a time in which change may be one of the few constants in their lives. These are assets, necessary, but not sufficient. Their digital experience and networking skills will need to become literacy in the use of technology, information, and media. Their comfort with diversity and globalization will have to grow into multicultural and interpersonal competence. And their demand for change will need to translate into a set of skills required to live in an era of continuing flux and to work for the changes they desire.

Their deficits are significant. This is a timid generation of rule followers in an era that demands bold, new rule makers. They are self-centered and have little experience with failure in what is likely to be period requiring flexibility, adaptation, and resilience. They are immature, needy, and tethered to the adults in their lives in a time that requires vision and leadership. They are tribal, self-centered, and low in interpersonal skills in an era that will be characterized by growing interconnectedness and mutual dependence. They are weak in basic skills in a developing information economy that will demand the highest levels of skills and knowledge in history. They confuse effort with excellence and quantity with quality in an age in which the economy elevates outcomes over process. They talk internationally but their focus is local and their knowledge of the world is poor in an age of globalization.

This should not be taken as a slap or dismissal of current undergraduates, harkening back to the old saw about students being so much better in my day. They were not. This generation of college students is no better and no worse than other generations but, like every generation before, they are different and will live in world demanding a different set of skills and knowledge to thrive. As a result, this generation requires a different brand of education that will enable them to attain their personal dreams and to serve the society they must lead. The education we offered to previous generations, whether successful or not, will not work for these students. Toward this end, we suggest colleges and universities develop programs to educate students for the twenty-first century.

Educating Today's College Students for the Twenty-First Century

Colleges must educate this generation of undergraduates to thrive in an era of continuing change—to live productive and successful lives as citizens, parents, spouses, neighbors, friends, coworkers, followers, and leaders who will be responsible for building the world in the decades after they graduate. We suggest colleges and universities develop a program for today's students rooted in the five realities that will dominate their lives. It might be called an education for the twenty-first century. This will be a real challenge for higher education because it may be even less well prepared for that world than its students.

Educate Students to Live in a Time of Profound Change

Periods of change demand three specific types of skills, which could be called the three Cs. The first is critical thinking, the ability to ask hard questions, the capacity to formulate and solve problems, and the balanced judgment necessary to make decisions and choices. This is essential in a world in flux in which information is multiplying geometrically, ideologies masquerade as facts, and hard policy choices need to be made by citizens. The second is creativity, which is also critical in an era of change when old answers don't work as well as they once did, social institutions appear to be broken, and a new world as yet inchoate and unknowable is developing. Students need the ability to think out of the box, to find innovative solutions to looming problems in a shifting environment, and to develop new rules to guide the future. The final skill is continual learning, the ability to continually renew one's skills and knowledge, which is mandatory in a time of unremitting change when the half-life of knowledge is growing shorter and shorter and new technologies are burgeoning.

Teaching these skills must occur during the undergraduate years. Updating the content and advancing those skills will occur throughout students' lives. They will return to colleges or other institutions offering postsecondary education for this purpose but they will ask not for the breadth-and-depth, fixed-time education that baccalaureate programs typically impart. Rather they will want "just in time" education, that is, to learn the specific skills and knowledge they need right now.

Educate Students for Life in a Digital Society

Colleges and universities are not prepared to do this now. They are far behind their students in this area. Higher education, similar to the nation's other major social institutions, was created for another time and needs to be refitted for today's high technology world. Chapter One described the resulting mismatch between the nation's analog universities and their digital students. As noted, a majority of undergraduates said their courses would be improved if they made greater use of technology, if their professors knew more about how to use technology, and if more of their classes made use of blended instruction, combining online and in-person classes (Undergraduate Survey; 2009). As noted, colleges need to prepare a generation of students who are not simply technology users but who are also literate in the use of technology, information, and media.

As pointed out as well, current undergraduates differ from their colleges on matters as fundamental as how they conceive of and use the physical campus and time. For the most part, universities operate in fixed locales, campuses, and on fixed calendars, semesters, and quarters with classes of fifty minutes three times per week. By contrast, digital natives live in an anytime and any-place world, operating twenty-four hours a day, seven days a week, unbounded by physical location.

There is also a divergence between higher education and digital natives on the goals of education. Universities focus on teaching, the process of education, exposing students to instruction for specific lengths of time, whereas digital natives are more concerned with the outcomes of education, learning, and the mastery of content in the manner of games.

Higher education and digital natives also favor different methods of instruction. Universities have historically emphasized passive means of instruction—lectures and books—whereas digital natives tend to be more active learners, preferring interactive, hands-on methods of learning such as case studies, field study, and simulations. Higher education gives preference to traditional media—print—and digital natives favor new media—the Internet.

This is mirrored in a split between professors and students, who approach knowledge in very different ways. Faculty members were described previously as hunters who search for and generate knowledge to answer their questions. Digital natives by contrast are gatherers, who wade through a sea of data available to them online to find the answers to their questions. The former is rooted in the disciplines and depth of knowledge whereas the latter is inter- or a-disciplinary with a focus on breadth.

They see the role of students in education in a polarized fashion. Higher education focuses on the individual. The ideal of a college was once described by President James Garfield as Mark

Hopkins, the nineteenth-century president of Williams College, at one end of a log and a student on the other. Digital natives are oriented more toward group learning and social networking, characterized by collaboration and sharing of content. This is causing an ethical challenge for universities, which under certain circumstances view collaboration as cheating and uncited content sharing as plagiarism.

These are substantial gaps, which are complicated by the disparities in the way colleges and digital learners see their roles in education. Higher education is provider driven in belief and practice. That is, the university through its faculty determines the curriculum, the content, the instructional methods, the study materials, and the class schedule. Digital natives tend to be consumer driven, preferring to choose if not the curriculum and content they wish to study, then the instructional method by which they learn best, the materials they use to learn, and the schedule by which they choose to study.

This is not the first time colleges and their students have been out of step. In the early nineteenth century as the industrial revolution mounted, colleges in the main clung stubbornly to their classical curriculums, rooted in the ancient trivium and quadrivium and outmoded methods of instruction. This was a time in which college enrollments actually declined and many institutions closed their doors. But bold colleges, such as Union in Schenectady, New York, which were among the earliest adopters of modern language, science, and engineering instruction, boomed in interest such that Union's enrollment topped Yale's and Harvard's combined.

In the current era, we will not see higher education enrollments drop because college is now essential for obtaining most well-paying jobs, although enrollments today are artificially inflated due the recession and there is likely to be an adjustment as the economy improves. However, tardiness in acting on the part

of colleges and universities will give impetus to the growth and
expansion of alternative higher education: for-profit and nontraditional educators who have been more successful in offering programs better geared to digital natives and their older counterparts.

Colleges and universities will experience increasing competition from the for-profit sector, which views higher education as
an industry ripe for remaking, much as health care was. It is seen
to be high in cost, poor in leadership, low in productivity, and
weak in technology use. It also has a set of virtues that make it
even more appealing to the business sector. Higher education is a
growth industry with dependable cash flows, has long-term sales,
receives payment prior to providing its services, is countercyclical
in revenues, and is subsidized by the government.

At the same time, we are witnessing a convergence of
knowledge-producing and -distributing organizations that are
entering the higher education marketplace—museums, libraries, media companies, software and game makers, zoos, and
symphony orchestras, to name just a few. This will create further competition for higher education as these organizations seek
to reach larger audiences, using technologies similar to those
employed by higher education, and producing products that look
increasingly like courses. The fields of education and management
have been two of the most popular areas of overlap and a number
of these organizations are gaining degree-granting status.

So colleges must change because of increasing competition but
even more so because their students need a different brand of education. The digital revolution is not a passing fad and students are
not going to change, so their colleges must.

It is important to ask how much colleges and universities will
be required to change. In 1828, facing industrialization and a
Connecticut legislature that disapproved of Yale's classical curriculum, the Yale faculty responded with a report that in part asked
whether the college needed to change a lot or a little. They said

this was the wrong question. The question that should be asked is what is the purpose of a college? This remains the right question today.

The purposes of the university have not changed. They remain the preservation and advancement of knowledge and the education of our students for humane, productive, and satisfying lives in the world in which they will live. The activities of universities will continue to be teaching, research, and service.

What must change, however, is the means by which we educate the digital natives who are and will be sitting in our classrooms—employing calendars, locations, pedagogies, and learning materials consistent with the ways our students learn most effectively. It means that the curriculum must meet our students where they are, not where we hope they might be or where we are. All education is essentially remedial, teaching students what they do not know. This, for example, is a generation that is stronger in gathering than hunting skills. So let the curriculum begin with breadth and move to depth.

It doesn't make sense to tie education to a common process. Rooting education in a uniform amount of seat time being exposed to teaching and a fixed clock is outdated and no longer makes sense. We all learn at different rates. Each of us even learns different subject matters at different rates. As a consequence, higher education must in the years ahead move away from its emphasis on teaching to learning, from its focus on common processes to common outcomes. With this will come the possibility of offering students a variety of different ways to achieve those outcomes rooted in the ways they learn best, an approach Alverno College in Milwaukee embraced in 1973. Increasingly, government is demanding that colleges make this change.

The library must move from the periphery of the college campus to its center. It has to be transformed from a storehouse for content to the central campus authority on knowledge—the discovery, incubation, distribution, application, combination, and recombination of knowledge. Colleges and universities are populated by faculty members who are experts in content but they know relatively little about the structure and use of knowledge. Libraries will have to lead their campuses in this regard.

This is merely the task of taking an essential institution and maintaining its historic vitality. In an information economy, there is no more important social institution than the university in its capacity to fuel our economy, our society, and our minds. To accomplish this, the university must simultaneously be rooted in our past and our present with its vision on the future.

Every college and university needs to decide where it will stand on the digital spectrum. Will it be a brick institution (a college that focuses on campus life and close, face-to-face inter-action between the members of the college community), a click institution (a university that offers instruction and services largely online), or a brick-and-click college, combining both? Each of these types of institutions incorporates digital technology but uses it differently. At brick campuses, technology is a means of enriching, expediting, expanding, and supplementing face-to-face education by enhancing instruction, expanding services and resources available to the college community, and enlarging the scope and reach of the campus. At click campuses, technology is the primary means by which instruction, services, and resources are provided. Institutions choosing to be brick will need to be more brick than ever before, seeking to re-create the spirit of Mark Hopkins's log if they are to attract students given the wealth of cheaper alternatives available. Those universities that aspire to become click institutions will face stiff competition from for-profit higher education in an environment that will be characterized increasingly by the dominance of a small number of megaproviders. The most crowded space will be for brick-and-click higher education, where institutions must decide the appropriate balance between brick-and-click education and the audience for their programs.

Educate Students for Life in a Diverse, Global Society

Colleges and universities tend to address this issue under two separate banners: multiculturalism and globalization.

Multiculturalism   This subject, or what was called *diversity* in an earlier incarnation, has been on the higher education agenda for almost half a century. Over the years the focus has shifted from access and opportunity to retention and graduation; initially from blacks to people of all colors, genders, sexual orientations, and disabilities; from assimilation to celebration of differences; from admission to the whole college experience: academic and coccurricular programs, services, staffing, and the resources that colleges provide.

At a board of trustees' long-range planning exercise Arthur attended, a trustee of color and an alumnus of the college was justifiably irked that the topic of diversity had not come up all day. In fact, nearly all of the students on this campus, except for those from abroad, were white. A lively conversation followed on the difficulty of attracting students of color to the rural Appalachian campus, located in an overwhelmingly white community from which the college drew most of its students. Suggestions were offered for remedies such as recruiting from urban areas with large populations of color and offering full scholarships to attract students of color. The strategies didn't make much sense for this institution because rural colleges have not generally been successful in attracting and retaining urban students of color, particularly when they lack a critical mass of peers and this institution in particular already had a very large tuition discount rate and could not afford scholarships sufficient to build that critical mass.

This college suffered from a problem common to higher education. Because the topics of diversity and multiculturalism have been so heated on the nation's campuses, the practice has been for administrators to respond to them as a series of discrete challenges, to seek quick fixes to issues one by one as they emerge. If purple students want a purple studies program, provide it. If green students want a green counselor in the student affairs office, hire one. If turquoise students desire turquoise food in the cafeteria, serve it. If orange students ask for an orange student week, establish it.

Creating college policy case by case is a dangerous practice. If purple students have been granted an ethnic studies program, why shouldn't blue students get one, too? In a mitotic environment, when the dark purple or light purple students contained within the purple group demand a separate counselor, why shouldn't they have one? Allowing curriculums, cocurriculums, and services to be determined by political pressure rather than academic need is bad policy, particularly in hard financial times.

However, the nation and our campuses are changing with regard to multiculturalism. The nation's population is growing increasingly diverse; glass ceilings are being cracked, walls between diverse groups on campus are becoming more porous, populations within those groups are becoming more diverse, and students are more comfortable with differences. Eighty-three percent of college students say it is essential (40 percent) or fairly important (43 percent) for college to provide experiences with and understanding of people different from themselves in race, religion, place of origin, and so on (Student Affairs Survey, 2008).

This is the moment for colleges and universities with leadership from their presidents to do what they have long needed to do. They should define the meaning of diversity on their campuses, what their institution would look like if it were truly diverse. The definition will vary from campus to campus depending on their demographics. It would surely not mean the same thing for community colleges in Mississippi with its large African American population and their counterparts in New Mexico with its greater concentration of Hispanics and Native Americans.

Then colleges can turn their definitions into comprehensive plans for action, ranging across admissions, financial aid, academic offerings, cocurricular programs, facilities, staffing, services, and the rest. This plan can then be translated into calendars, budgets, and responsible parties.

The current mood on campus also makes this an excellent time for colleges, under the banner of embracing commonality and celebrating differences, to build bridges between diverse groups on campus in and out of the classroom, to demonstrate their commitment to support and provide comfort zones for diverse groups, and to educate students regarding the commonalities they share. This is also the right moment for colleges and universities to address the two already hottest diversity issues in higher education, sexual orientation and social class, if they have not already.

In their book, *21st Century Skills* authors Bernie Trilling and Charles Fadel identified a set of competencies student need with regard to diversity to be socially adept and crossculturally fluent. These include the ability to "interact effectively with others" (i.e., "know when it is appropriate to listen" and "when to speak and conduct themselves in a respectable, professional manner") and "work effectively in diverse teams" (i.e., "respect cultural differences and work effectively with people from a range of social and cultural backgrounds"; "respond open-mindedly to different ideas and values," and "leverage social and cultural differences to create new ideas, increase innovation, and quality of work") (Trilling & Fadel, 2009, p. 81). Students need to develop these skills.

Guided team projects in and out of class have proved an excellent way of building them. Two of the groups on many campuses that have been most successful in this regard are sports teams and theater groups. The simple fact is that even if the quarterback is black and the halfback is white, they need each other to score a touchdown. With theater groups, if Romeo is gay and Juliet is straight, they still need to act as if they are deeply in love for their performance to be compelling. In groups that work closely together and are mutually dependent, people get to know each other as people rather than through the lens of their differences alone. Creating diverse student problem-solving groups is a powerful pedagogical tool for building bridges and also critically important for a job market that increasingly demands it.

The basic issues with regard to diversity in higher education have not changed though progress has been made in many spheres. There continue to be too many missing persons at America's colleges and universities, populations that are underrepresented in their student bodies, faculties, and administrations. Graduation rates for students from underrepresented populations and tenure rates for faculty members from those groups are still too low. Though students of color are more satisfied with their college experience than their predecessors, too many still feel as uncomfortable on campus as do white and Asian American students with regard to issues of diversity. They have little knowledge of the various civil rights movements that occurred before they were born. The curriculum, although more multicultural than in the past, is still in need of greater multicultural content, not because it is politically correct but because that is the heritage and the future of this nation. Colleges need to push harder in these areas through programming for students and faculty development initiatives. Numbers can be enhanced if colleges and universities reduce merit-based financial aid in favor of need-based aid. Government financial aid is also key here.

Globalization   Globalization is a far newer issue for colleges and universities, yet all or nearly all of the institutions we visited were in the process of making their campuses more international, even two-year colleges where the focus is more on the local community. These efforts were largely incremental and extraordinarily wide ranging. Institutions were engaged in a grab bag of activities, including augmenting their existing classes, adding new courses, mounting new area studies and language programs, enrolling more international students, expanding study abroad opportunities for their own students, employing greater numbers of international faculty and having more of their own staff teach in other countries, creating exchange programs with universities around the globe, offering their programs, even establishing campuses abroad, and growing their cocurricular and residential programs. Their libraries have added more international resources, food services have expanded their menus, new student clubs have been created, research centers have multiplied, and the number of international speakers and events have grown.

The internationalization of higher education is inevitable. We will get there by successive approximations, which is the way in which American higher education has historically met new challenges. This nation's universities evolved from classical colleges through this process over the course of a half-century. A model research university, Johns Hopkins, was even established in Baltimore in 1876.

The same is likely to occur with regard to globalization. If history is a guide, most universities will continue to make gradual changes toward internationalization. Some will serve as leaders, making globalization a primary focus of their activities. The most elite universities are likely to act as legitimizers, adopting and advocating the most successful of the changes pioneered at other institutions. There could also be a new university, which serves as a model, though it may not be an American university.

Today, we don't know what an international university looks like. However, colleges and universities need to go beyond drift and accretion. As with diversity, this is a time to plan, establish goals for international education, and create the academic and cocurricular programs necessary to achieve those goals. This is essential because our students are a generation who will live in a flattening world and lack even basic knowledge about it. As noted, although undergraduates certainly feel they are members of a global society, they do not recognize the names of the leaders who are playing such a critical role in it now. This generation requires an education that will provide them with the knowledge they lack; an understanding of the global nature of politics, economics, technology, geography, social relationships, culture, language, religion, ethics, and more; and the skills and knowledge necessary to live successful lives in that world. Three out of five undergraduates surveyed believe undergraduate education would be improved if all students were required to take courses examining other cultures (Undergraduate Survey, 2009).

Education for Life in an Evolving Information Economy

Undergraduates need an education that will prepare them in the short run for an economy in recession and in the longer term for a developing information economy in which they will have an average of six different careers, some of which may not yet exist. The education for both is the same. It includes an enriched major, practical minors, internships, and puts career counseling on steroids.

The Enriched Major   At the core of education for an information economy is an enriched version of the major. It would go beyond the traditional design of undergraduate majors to include a broader, more interdisciplinary base; an emphasis on teaching not only the skills traditionally associated with a discipline but also the twenty-first-century skills that have been discussed; and application of skills and content to problem solving.

We live in an interdisciplinary world that cannot be viewed adequately through the lens of a single discipline. The argument for disciplinary majors has been that they provide students with a deep body of knowledge and the skills to advance, question, and keep vital that body of knowledge. This remains essential today, but it is no longer sufficient. Students need a broader more interdisciplinary view of the world. The enriched major should study the roots and values of a student's concentration including its history, ethical foundation, standards, limits and limitations, points of agreement and disagreement, and how differences are resolved or accommodated. It should contrast a student's concentration to other disciplines in their study of common problems, demonstrating similarities and differences in worldview, modes of inquiry, standards of evidence, uses and abuses, and values. It should apply the concentration to the great challenges of our time such as globalization, the evolution of the information economy, the diversity of our society, and the technology revolution.

The enriched major might begin with an interdisciplinary class bringing together students contemplating different majors to focus on a single problem led by faculty members from different disciplines and conclude with a course in the senior year with a similar design but in which the responsibility for solving the problem rests with the students. The interdisciplinary perspective would continue throughout the whole of the undergraduate experience.

In this environment, the body of knowledge students are asked to learn in their majors will have a shorter half-life than it has had historically. Arthur tells the story of having taken a graduate seminar on the cell membrane during his senior year of college in which three competing theories were tested. He didn't learn which theory had gained currency until he read his daughter's eighth-grade biology textbook years later. More than ever before students need to master the skills by which they can remain current in their fields. This is true even though those skills will age as well as the content they studied and will need continual upgrading. Mastery of the three Cs will be a distinct plus here.

Beyond this, students need to learn the skills that are required by today's workplaces and that are already being employed by many faculty members in their own work. These include the ability to work in teams and diverse groups; being adaptable, flexible, and resilient; acquiring problem-solving skills; being responsible, independent, and accountable; and developing leadership capabilities. Several of these areas are specific needs for a generation of students who have had little experience with failure, are more dependent on their parents than their predecessors, spend much of their time in the comfort zone of a tribe, and are rule followers. Because they are also gatherers of information, most likely to turn to *Wikipedia* for their research, they need to develop the skills essential to engage in deep, concentrated research, the hunting skills. Colleges and universities would be doing a service to these students if they deflated their grading systems. This is a generation that has grown accustomed to consistent affirmation and approval, a common complaint by their employers, and they need a more realistic assessment of their strengths and weakness. The attributes listed here should be taught in every class a university offers, but the major, with its interconnected series of courses and increasing levels of expectation from introductory to advanced instruction, offers a particularly good opportunity to progressively develop student skills in these areas.

The major should also provide an opportunity to apply the skills and knowledge students have learned. Guided internship and service experiences linking academic and field-based education as well as classes that employ problem-solving pedagogies, capstone courses, and senior projects provide excellent vehicles for accomplishing this. They also have the virtue of making students more employable.

Practical Minors   Students are double majoring in order gain an edge in the job market, which reduces college simply to classes in their twin areas of concentration and general education requirements. They don't need to do this. A minor in a second field will serve them just as well. Colleges can help students in this regard by creating an array of practical minors, four to five courses, in what even may be cognate areas. For instance, the art major could be offered a minor in scientific illustration or the English major could take a minor in technical writing or the psychology major could enroll in a cluster of courses in human resources management. A great number of the courses necessary to establish such programs already exist on many campuses. Even at liberal arts colleges, which may lack professional programs, such courses can be combinations of classes from different disciplines and a newly developed course integrating them. The practical minor can have great appeal in the workplace, particularly if augmented by internships, service experiences, and senior projects related to that minor.

Guided internships of a semester's length or more, which integrate class work with experience, are an important part of the undergraduate education. Academically, they provide students with an opportunity to apply what they have learned in the classroom and to test career interests. Faculty members commonly find that students returning from internships, able to better understand the connections between theory and practice, are intellectually more curious and demanding in class. Practically, internships are a career plus, giving students experience in the field in which they will seek employment, which is very attractive to employers. They are in addition appealing to perspective students and their parents in the college-selection process, particularly at liberal arts colleges, which have tended to be less career oriented.

Career Services   Typically college students begin to use career services offices in their senior year when they are on the job market. The recession has brought them in earlier but primarily to find jobs and paying internships to cover college expenses. In today's difficult and changing economy, this use of career services is too late and too little. Comprehensive career programs need to be offered to students and their parents from the first days of college. Given that only a minority of students are active in campus life, this means career counseling cannot be relegated to an isolated campus office.

It should be a part of orientation for all students and interested parents. At most institutions, this is one of the rare occasions in which attendance is allegedly mandatory and colleges have the relatively full attention of what are often frightened students about to start a new life. A required first-year experience course, an element of an enriched major, could build on this, focusing on life planning, future careers, the context of change in which they will work, the place of work in a full and rich life, and practical matters such as how to write a résumé, find jobs, and interview for them. The foundation is already there for doing this. More than a third of community college students (36 percent) and a majority of undergraduates at four-year colleges (53 percent) are already taking such courses (Undergraduate Survey, 2009). This class, which should be credit bearing, can be extended through a student's entire undergraduate career.

Colleges and universities can also better serve their students and some already are by having career services reach out to them individually and personally, which is simpler with a first-year-experience course requiring students to make an appointment with career counseling; linking career counseling with academic advising, making explicit the career competencies associated with each courses as well as cocurricular programs and creating transcripts for recording them; and offering career assistance to students after graduation via networking, social media, and podcasts.

These would be wonderful benefits for a pragmatic career-oriented generation desperate to achieve the American Dream, who are now choosing careers too often not because they want to work in the field, but because they believe the employment prospects better.

Education for Civic Engagement

Societies require that their members have a shared body of knowledge to function. Current undergraduates have glaring gaps in their cultural knowledge and even larger gaps in their intercultural knowledge. Even more troubling, the astronomical number and variety of information sources available to us and our differential use of them is quickly reducing the possibility of a common body of cultural knowledge.

In order to compensate, we suggest that colleges and universities provide students with a common general education that links past and present, our heritage with the realities that face us. This general education program, also suggested in *When Hope and Fear Collide*, would have five components. It differs from the traditional general education program in that it is not rooted in the familiar disciplines and subject matters, but rather in the shared human experience. It is a program designed specifically to prepare current undergraduates for the lives they will live and the world they will inhabit. It seeks to marry intellectual vitality, which must be intrinsic to academe, with the practical education students so urgently need today.

Communication Skills   The first of the skills and knowledge areas is communication. At the most basic level, current students need to be fluent in two languages: words and numbers. All learning is premised on mastery of these subjects. For a generation that is weak in both languages, it is essential that each be included in the college curriculum. It is also vital that students learn a third language, symbols. Via the arts, we communicate as powerfully as through words and numbers, touching our senses, emotions, and intellect. One clarification is in order. In a global era, we would be remiss if we left the impression that words meant only English. Although the rest of the world seems to be mastering English, it is important that students become literate in another language, which offers an extraordinary tool for learning about how other cultures think and view the world.

Human Heritage   The second element is the study of human heritage, true hope, not the Pollyannish variety but the sort rooted in conviction and grounded optimism, demands an understanding of the past as well as the present. Society, in the words of Edmund Burke, is a contract "not only between those who are living, but between those who are living, those who are dead and those who are to be born (Burke, 1967, p. 318). The goal in studying human heritage is not for students to memorize a list of great names and key dates but rather to understand how societies and their populations have responded to an ever-changing economic, technological, demographic, and social world. Only if we can teach students about the successes and failures and the rises and declines of humanity can their dreams, aspirations, and fears be realistically grounded.

In the past, this was accomplished by teaching undergraduates about the United States and the western world. This is no longer sufficient. Today in a flat, global society, an education that does not include seminal works such as the *Koran* cannot be considered complete. Students must learn about the nations and leaders who shaped the world yesterday, today, and have the capacity to shape tomorrow's.

The Environment The third element is education regarding the environment in which students will live their lives. This "green" generation needs to understand the natural environment and the handmade environment in which they live and take responsibility for nurturing each.

With regard to the natural environment, students need to become literate scientifically; they need to know the basic facts and ways of thinking that constitute science. They must come to understand the inhabitants, planet, and universe in which we live. They need to be educated to become effective citizens, to learn about the public policy choices they will need to make and the criteria for making those choices.

With regard to the human-made environment, the agenda is larger and even more difficult. Ralph Waldo Emerson wrote, "We do not make a world of our own, but fall into institutions already made and have to accommodate ourselves to them . . . (Emerson, 1926, p. 55). Current undergraduates are actively engaged in community service but they are negative about the institutions on which their communities depend and the people who lead them. They are optimistic about their personal futures and pessimistic about the future of the country. To counter the rising disenchantment and disengagement of current students from government and our other social institutions, they need to learn what those social institutions—political, cultural, aesthetic, economic, educational, and spiritual—were created to accomplish. Students should learn how these institutions came into being, how they evolved over time, how they function and malfunction, how they impose obligations, how they can be held accountable, and how they can be changed.

Individual Roles The individual, but multifaceted roles that all human beings play in life—friend, family member, worker, citizen, leader, and follower—is the fourth element of the program. They must understand the nature of relationships, the choices they can make, the expectations associated with each role, the ways in which balance can be achieved among the various roles, and the part each role plays in creating a full and complete life. They need the skills, knowledge, and experience to perform each role. To understand these is essential if students are to develop a sense of efficacy and authority, critical for a generation so closely tied to their parents and so slow to take responsibility for their lives. It is a must for a generation that believes an individual can make a difference but is torn between doing well and doing good. This is the core of the career planning and preparation that today's students need and could form the foundation of the first-year college experience course proposed previously.

Values   The fifth and final element of general education is values. This is critically important if students are to gain an appreciation of differences, respect other people, or understand why plagiarism is wrong. Bertrand Russell made explicit why this is essential when he wrote, "Without civic morality, communities perish; without personal morality, their survival has no meaning" (Russell, 1949, p. 355). Students must learn the meaning of values, be able to distinguish between values and facts, understand the difference between relative and absolute values, and differentiate among good, better, and best. They also need to develop mechanisms for weighing and choosing among values. Finally they need to understand how values fit into our lives, the changing nature of values over time, how cultures define and regulate values, the place of values in an individual's life, and what happens to minority values in society.

In sum, this general education program is intended not merely as remediation for a generation of students who know too little about the world in which they live, but more to provide today's undergraduates with a common vocabulary and a shared body of knowledge. It is to cement connections in a world in which our differences increasingly overshadow our commonalities. This has been essential in every generation but it is mandatory for citizenship in the twenty-first century, for an era demanding hard decisions that require higher levels of knowledge and skills of their citizens than ever before.

Education for the Twenty-First Century

We have proposed an education to prepare students for the twenty-first century. It is grounded in our shared heritage, language, natural and human-made environment, and values. It is rooted in the challenges that face us, providing education for a period of profound change, an era of digital transformation, an epoch of growing diversity and globalization, an age of evolution in the information economy, and the continuing need for an engaged citizenry. It seeks to counter student weaknesses, enhance their strengths, and develop the skills, knowledge, and dispositions necessary in the years ahead.

This proposal is not only about subject matter and content. It is also about pedagogy. We know that there is a mismatch between how professors teach and how their students learn. The education being suggested seeks to marry the two approaches, that is, integrating concrete and abstract knowledge acquired through active and passive methods of learning. This is not a suggestion of compromise so that students and professors each get something. It is a matter of students needing both things: concrete and abstract knowledge and the ability to learn actively and passively. To accomplish this, the classics need to be augmented with case studies, the classroom needs to be supplemented with field experience, and research by hunting must be joined with research by gathering. The Internet needs to replace the blackboard.

The education being proposed needs to go beyond the formal curriculum. It should infuse all aspects of collegiate life. The goals should be reinforced in the awards that an institution gives, in the speakers who are invited to campus, in the few widely attended events such as orientation and graduation, in the publications an institution produces, in the services students are provided, and in the activities in which students are involved. With students spending less time on campus and being less involved in campus activities, it is essential that colleges recognize that they have few opportunities to educate them outside the classroom and use those times to focus on their most important lessons.

Undergraduate education has changed dramatically over its 375-year history in this country to meet the twin needs of remaining intellectually vital and providing useful and practical education. Whenever societies change quickly, there is a tendency for the college curriculum to lose these anchor points. In a short time, a course of studies can become obsolete. It no longer prepares students for the world in which they will live and it imparts an intellectual tradition that has become stale and dated.

As discussed, the nineteenth century was such a time in which the classical curriculum of agrarian America gave way to a curriculum better fitted to an industrial age with its focus on breadth, specialization, the disciplines, and the professions. Today, our society is being transformed once again, which requires us to develop a new vision of education that will prepare our students for the emerging world and the relentless pace of change they will encounter throughout their lives as they move from the 1.0 to 2.0 digital worlds and perhaps beyond. This proposal is offered in the hope that it might aid in this process.

Employing Today's College Students

In the course of writing this book, we discussed our findings with perhaps two dozen people who employ this generation of college graduates. They were from small and large organizations, for profit and not for profit, in different parts of the country. Their reactions were roughly the same: head nodding, often vigorous, smiles, and cutting us off to confirm what we had found and to add their own anecdotes. They told us, "They are the worst employees I have ever hired"; "I try not to hire them"; "I don't understand them"; "we had to change many of our personnel practices"; and "they know more about technology than I will ever know."

They described a generation of employees who have the following characteristics:

- Expect to be rewarded for showing up
- Want the keys to the kingdom on day one
- Ask for a raise after a month of mediocre performance
- E-mail to say they are working at home because it is such a beautiful day
- Request an extended lunch the first week on the job to go shopping with friends
- Immediately call their bosses by their first names
- Can't tolerate ambiguity and need to be told exactly what to do repeatedly
- Don't see the big picture
- Don't care about customers
- Quit with little or no notice after short periods on the job
- Can't write a letter and can't do the basic math of making change
- Dress inappropriately
- Are always on social networks instead of working
- Think they are smarter than the experienced older adults they work for
- Can't take criticism and are defensive

- Assume the nice things that are done for them are owed to them

- Ask parents to fight their battles

- Don't meet deadlines and expect to work nine to five

However, employers acknowledge that these graduates are smart, understand technology in ways their employers often don't, have skills with social media that their organizations greatly need today, are used to working in teams, and are aware, tolerant, and even encouraging of change.

None of this is surprising. This is a generation that does feel entitled, expect approbation, have weak basic skills and large knowledge gaps, confuse effort with quality, multitask, follow rules, and blur the boundaries between their social and work lives. They are college graduates who want balance between their jobs and personal lives, want relationships with their employers, want to be listened to and do not want to fail, which helps to explain why they are rule followers, deal poorly with ambiguity, and seek parental intervention.

So what should employers do? A few of the smaller organizations we spoke with said they try to avoid hiring recent college graduates in favor of older adults who come without some of their baggage. Most organizations cannot and should not do this. They need employees who come with the strengths this generation brings and in information economies, talent is key.

There are some strategies that can help close the gap. The first is to identify potential future hires early and offer them internships and summer jobs. It is a useful way to introduce current students to the organizational culture, the expectations of the employer, the work, and the people. This serves as a useful screening device for future employees, a vehicle for assessing the organization's strengths and weaknesses in the eyes of today's college students, a good laboratory for evaluating the characteristics to seek in successful future

employees, and a tool to reduce employee attrition by giving potential hires a better sense of what they are getting into.

Second, provide new employees with an extended orientation
before beginning their jobs. This is the time to be explicit about
expectations, promotion, work rules, evaluation, job hours, social
media usage, dress codes, telecommuting, and all the other details
that may not have been necessary in the past. Codify the rules in
much the way that professors are doing with syllabi. Consider
opening a portion of that orientation to parents, detailing what
their children will be doing and the appropriate role of parents in
the organization, even if it's none.

Third, customize job descriptions to specific employees and
make evaluation frequent, constructive, and the criteria explicit.
Consider hiring employees for three-month probationary periods
in which assessment is built in biweekly.

Fourth, determine which current organizational practices are
essential. Give particular attention to flexible hours, telecommuting, dress codes, use of first names, parent services, and the notion
of supervisors as coaches.

Fifth, there are some don'ts. Don't assume new employees
are self-starters or self-motivated. Both need to be fueled and
stoked. Don't assume new employees know what is and is not
appropriate. Don't assume employees know what to do on even
simple tasks. Show them and grow their jobs and responsibilities
over time.

Sixth, set high expectations and hold employees accountable
for achieving them. Provide regular training to help make this
possible. Think about incorporating games, problem solving, and
team work into training.

Seventh, this generation comes with real assets that many
older adults lack. Don't squander them. Solicit counsel from digital natives but don't ask for feedback unless you are prepared to
listen to it and use it. If not used, explain why.

Eighth, sign up for a gym if you employ recent college graduates, especially if you are a baby boomer for whom the mismatch
is greatest. The gym is a better stress reliever than alcohol, scream-
ing, or kicking the dog. Recent college graduates respond even
more poorly to yelling and sarcasm than the rest of us.

Parenting Today's College Students

Logically, this section would have preceded colleges and employers but it was necessary to introduce the ghost of Christmas
present—the children parents are sending to college and the ghost
of Christmas future—the experience employers are having with
their children after college before talking about Christmas past—
the parenting of today's college students. This is a departure from
Dickens but a necessary one in this case.

Parents have raised and by all reports are continuing to raise a
generation of children who have the characteristics that have been
described. They are entitled, overprotected, timid, dependent, self-
absorbed, rule followers, tied to their parents, and have not been
allowed to fail. This has not happened because they have bad parents. Rather parents have attempted to compensate for past and
present circumstances. Many of the fathers and mothers of today's
college students are baby boomers, who were divided from their
parents by their politics and lifestyle. They have tried to develop
better relationships with their kids than they had. Some have
sought to become more like friends than parents.

A higher proportion of their children have lived in single-parent
families. In a majority of families, both parents have worked. As a
result the dads and moms have attempted to make up for the time
away from their children by lavishing all they can on them and
keeping in contact as much as possible, which is made far easier
by digital communications. They have only wanted the best for
their kids—the best schools, the best colleges, the best lives. Many

assisted their children with the homework, school projects, tutoring, enrichment activities, and more. They did all they could to eliminate the possibility of failure and rewarded their children for trying. They created a "Lake Wobegon" environment in which all children were special, "above average," and the children believed it.

Parents sought to protect their children in a world that may have seemed more dangerous than in the era when they grew up. For some, this meant attempting to build a cocoon or safety net around their kids, to save them from the hurts they experienced. They wanted to avoid preventable skinned knees. One area in which they were less successful was preventing access to inappropriate digital content and potentially abusive social media users, activities the kids were more knowledgeable about than many of their parents. New problems like cyberbullying and sexting were beyond the ken of many. Alcohol, sex, and drugs too often lacked sufficient vigilance.

Today's future college students need to grow up with loving and caring parents who will enable them to live full, satisfying, and successful lives in the twenty-first century, not friends. This means teaching children right from wrong in regards to words and deeds. It means reading to them, talking to them, listening to them, and caring for them.

It also means preparing children to be independent. Assisting them when they are young to make small decisions and supporting them as they grow older in making larger ones. It means not answering all of an adolescent's questions, but directing them increasingly as they age to the resources to find the answers themselves.

It means building responsibility and accountability in children. This is a gradual process that involves asking children to be responsible for jobs around the house rather than doing those jobs for them. It is having the child sell cookies for the class trip door to door rather than selling them at the office. It is supporting children in school assignments rather than doing the work for them. It is having children clean up their own messes in school or with the neighbors rather than patching it over for them. The parent should be an advocate, a coach, and a source of solace, but not a fixer. The leash we have to our children should grow longer as they demonstrate responsibility. Here Ronald Reagan's dictum of trust but verify is wholly appropriate. Young adults need to develop autonomy, to become adept at dealing with the feelings, problems, and worries they have throughout the day rather than immediately calling, texting, and e-mailing home for solutions. Tenacity, patience, and an ability solve problems is essential.

It means making children resilient by allowing for controlled failures with parental support after. Children should not be given unconditional applause for everything they do, just unconditional love. They need honest, encouraging, and caring feedback on what they have done well and what they have not. To develop imagination and confidence, children need encouragement to take safe risks, and as they get older to be encouraged to try less-safe but intelligent risks that will stretch them.

It means helping children develop empathy for others, taking them out of their comfort zone, and seeing how other people with less live their lives and having them earn the discretionary material possessions they receive rather than feeling they are entitlements. It means enabling them to develop interpersonal skills that go beyond their circle and tribe.

It means teaching children about sharing and giving. Parents need to model this behavior and children should begin to give a portion of what they have to others who need it at early ages. They should begin to participate in service activities when they are young, not to pad their credentials for college, but because it is a fundamental human responsibility.

It means establishing limits. Inappropriate content and mis-use of the Internet should be barred. Access should be controlled.

Children need education and clear rules regarding drugs, sex, and alcohol. Parents must construct floors of acceptable behavior and with their children build the superstructure.

If parents help their children develop independence, responsibility, accountability, resilience, industry, confidence, creativity, empathy, interpersonal skills, altruism, and a sense of discipline, they will have given them an extraordinary gift, the basic skills and values to thrive in the twenty-first century and to parent their own children.

Civically Engaging Today's College Students

For democratic societies to survive, they need an engaged and educated citizenry. Today's college students are not well educated regarding civic affairs and most report they are disenchanted with government and do not believe the US political system can solve the nation's problems.

Yet, today's college students are actually highly engaged in civic life through the service activities they perform. But they would be unlikely to characterize their activities in this fashion. They view service in very personal terms, people helping people rather than as matters of policy, politics, or institutions. This is a critical distinction that allows current college students to retreat from government but continue to serve their neighbors. Civic engagement and altruism are not synonymous, particularly if those involved don't see the connection. When college students were asked the best way to solve the important issues facing the country, community volunteerism (36 percent) beat political engagement (26 percent) and "don't know" edged them both out (37 percent) (Institute of Politics, 2011).

But government has the capacity to join them. President Kennedy did this more than half a century ago by summoning the nation to build a "new frontier." He told Americans they had a responsibility to give to their country. His creation of the Peace Corps (a federal volunteer program designed to provide technical assistance abroad, help people in other countries better understand the United States, and enable Americans to learn about other cultures) modeled that expectation.

Our situation is similar today. We stand at the edge of a new frontier, as America races toward global, digital, information economy 2.0. Once again, young people can be challenged to ask what they can do for their country.

It is possible to create a Peace Corps for the current generation of college students. A majority said they would be willing to engage in a year or two of community service or teaching in exchange for a reduction in college costs. The country needs the volunteers and Teach For America, which enlists high-ability college graduates to teach in high-need schools, demonstrates what is possible. It attracts the most-able college graduates in the country to perform service as teachers in high-need schools. It makes teaching, which this group of college graduates traditionally bypasses because of its low salaries and lack of prestige, alluring and high status. Its alumni have a record of continuing service to the country.

The base for such a program already exists in AmeriCorps, a federal domestic service program that provides volunteers with a living allowance and college support. However, AmeriCorps currently lacks the stature, reputation, and desirability of Teach For America, even though AmeriCorps helps to support it and service activities across the country. What is being suggested is a highly visible, highly prestigious, highly appealing, and highly selective version of AmeriCorps. These were the characteristics of the original Peace Corps, which not only provided service opportunities to a relatively small number of people but also made service glamorous, inextricably connected service with civic engagement, and excited the imagination of the country. We need that today.

In today's poor economy, such a program would also have the virtues of reducing student indebtedness following college and decreasing the number of college graduates entering the job market, which was the reason for creating the original GI Bill in 1944. The goal was not so much to increase college attendance by veterans but to get them off the labor market. For these reasons, a new Peace Corps would enable college students to do good and to do well.

Beyond such a signature program, the digital tools for engaging young people in civic affairs are far more powerful than media were fifty years ago. Communication can be targeted, individualized, and interactive, which is a distinct advantage for a generation that is issue oriented rather than ideological. But more than this, social media promise disintermediation between the candidate and the voter. Nowhere are the prospects more apparent than in the music industry, which has experienced profound disintermediation between the "talent" and the consumer. One of the appeals to young people of President Obama's 2008 campaign is that it seemed a grassroots, bottom-up effort. Social media provided a direct link between young people and Senator Obama, absent the countless layers of bureaucracy that surround a candidate. It is an increasing expectation on the part of young people that they will have "personal" relationships with the significant people in their lives. Politics is becoming an increasingly retail business for young people

In contrast to candidates, government appears to be top down. However, participation can be enlarged, interaction can be increased, and decision making might even be improved via mechanisms such as blogging, virtual town halls, crowd sourcing, and online voting. The public can be asked about how well a law is working or expertise can be amassed to solve problems. Today's college students want to be listened to and when their counsel is not adopted, they want to know why. Transparency is important to them.

But all of this is mechanics. In one of the focus-group interviews, a student recounted the old chestnut, "How can you tell when a politician is lying? His lips move." Integrity and competence are desperately needed in government. They are prerequisites to civic engagement by young people in an age when news reports are filled with accounts of the failure of both. One student told us he learned what a blow job was in elementary school. His teacher was the president of the United States.

In the end, civic engagement rests on government's ability to serve the people's needs and for government officers to honestly and effectively do the people's work. It is critical to college students that government preserve and champion the American Dream, that fairness and opportunity, which they believe to be badly skewed today, be restored for all. They believe neither is happening today. For this generation, jaded with regard to politicians and political rhetoric, government calls for idealism and increased civic participation have to be matched by proof of action. Gridlock and the inability of government to function make such words seem cynical and empty, if not outright lies.

One of the most tangible ways in which government can match rhetoric and reality is to make its promise of college access and graduation a reality for all capable Americans. In 1947, President Truman's Commission on Higher Education for Democracy recommended making a minimum of two years of tuition-free college available to all capable Americans, increasing financial aid, making possible not only college access but also college choice, and ending the racial, religious, economic, geographic, and gender barriers to college access, among many other things (President's Commission on Higher Education, 1947).

We have made progress on this agenda, but not enough, and in some areas we are losing ground. Although the barriers of religion and gender have been broken, there continue to be substantial barriers with regard to race, economics, and geography.

Access to college is being limited by rising costs, the failure of financial aid to keep pace with prices, and the lack of sufficient higher education to serve growing populations in states such as California, where underrepresented populations are greatest and growing most quickly. In addition, changes in financial aid policy and practice such as the shifts from grants to loans and from need to merit-based aid serve to limit attendance by underrepresented populations. The goal of choice—permitting students to attend the institution that best matches their abilities and needs rather than the cheapest or closest—has never been a reality for most undergraduates and is declining as a possibility today.

These realities need to be reversed because they are governmental promises unfulfilled in a time when trust is low, the expectation is that government will not deliver, and undergraduates believe the resources of the country are unfairly and inequitably divided. They also need to be reversed because it is immoral for children to be denied the opportunity for college and the American Dream on the day they are born based on their parents' income or skin color. It also makes sense financially to reverse them if we are to preserve our democratic society, keep the United States competitive in the world, encourage economic growth, and make young people gainfully employable.

———

We know who today's college students are. We know the challenges they will face. We know the skills, knowledge, and attitudes this will require. In the years to come, our educational system, employers, parents, and government will be judged by their success in enabling today's undergraduates to live, work, and lead in a diverse, global, digital, information economy in motion. This generation of college students and their successors will be tested by their capacity to thrive in this environment. And the future of our nation and our world will be dependent on both.

Note

1. The focus is on higher education, employers, parents, and
   government because these are the institutions that were most
   germane to today's college students. Powerful cases could
   have been made for including religious institutions, schools,
   communities, and social organizations.

The Life and Times of the Class of 2012

A CHRONOLOGY

They were born in 1990, the year Iraq invaded Kuwait; East and West Germany reunified; the dismantling of the Soviet Union continued; President Bush broke a campaign promise of no new taxes; the Savings and Loan Crisis occurred in which nearly a quarter of nation's savings and loans failed, requiring a federal bailout; and investment bank Drexel Burnham Lambert defaulted on $100 million in loans.

They turned one in 1991 when US Operation Desert Storm drove Iraqi troops from Kuwait; unemployment hit the highest levels in twenty years; Boris Yeltsin was elected president of Russia; Clarence Thomas was named to the US Supreme Court, after prolonged hearings on charges of sexual harassment; and the first web browser was created.

They were two years old in 1992 when the Soviet Union ceased to exist; Russia and the United States signed the Strategic Arms Reduction Treaty and announced the end of the Cold War; rioting in Los Angeles followed a not-guilty verdict of police officers in the Rodney King trial; the Americans with Disabilities Act went into effect; texting began; and Bill Clinton was elected president of the United States.

They were three in 1993 when terrorists bombed New York City's World Trade Center; the "don't ask, don't tell" policy, mandating that the military not ask or require personnel to reveal their sexual orientation, was adopted; and the first smartphone was introduced.

They were four in 1994 when the web browser Netscape Navigator was created; Nelson Mandela was sworn in as president of South Africa; Rwanda suffered a one-hundred-day genocide in which eight hundred thousand people were killed; and the North American Free Trade Agreement went into effect.

They were five and entered kindergarten in 1995 when the DVD was developed; the five-year dot-com bubble began; the Oklahoma City federal building was bombed by American terrorists, in the deadliest terrorist attack to date in US history, killing 168 people and injuring 450; NATO intervened to stop the genocide in Bosnia; Yahoo! was founded; and the Dow Jones Index hit 4000.

They were seven in 1997 when the first Harry Potter book was published; the Northern Ireland Peace Accords were signed; Hong Kong returned to Chinese sovereignty; Princess Diana died in a car crash; and the Kyoto Protocol on Climate set binding targets on greenhouse emissions for thirty-seven industrial nations.

They were eight in 1998 when President Clinton was impeached in a sex scandal on charges of perjury and obstruction of justice; University of Wyoming student Matthew Shepard was tortured and murdered because he was gay; and Google was incorporated.

They were nine in 1999 when President Clinton was acquitted; two students killed thirteen and wounded twenty-one others at Columbine High School in Colorado; New York City police fired forty-one shots, killing an unarmed Guinean immigrant, Amadou Diallo; the euro came into being; and Napster, permitting peer-to-peer music sharing, was launched.

They were ten in 2000 when a Supreme Court decision ruled George Bush, who won the electoral college vote but lost the popular vote, had been elected the forty-third president of the United States and the human genome was decoded.

They were eleven in 2001 when al-Qaeda terrorists flew hijacked jumbo jets into the two World Trade Center towers and the Pentagon killing nearly three thousand people; the United States invaded Afghanistan, which harbored al-Qaeda cells; the War on Terror began and the USA PATRIOT ("Uniting and Strengthening America by Providing Appropriate Tools Required to Intercept and Obstruct Terrorism") Act became law; Enron, one of the world's leading energy companies, declared bankruptcy owing to massive accounting fraud; and the iPod was released.

They were twelve in 2002 when Guantanamo Bay detention camp for Afghan prisoners was established.

They were thirteen in 2003 when the United States went to war with Iraq over weapons of mass destruction, which were never found; the space shuttle *Columbia* broke apart while returning to earth; war began in Dafur; and Skype and Myspace were launched.

They were fourteen in 2004 when Facebook came into being; Massachusetts became the first state to legalize same-sex marriage; prisoner human rights violations were reported at Abu Ghraib prison in Iraq; and terrorist bombs on the Madrid commuter railroad killed 191 and wound 1,800.

They were fifteen and began high school in 2005 when Hurricane Katrina devastated New Orleans and the Gulf states; terrorists bombed the London Underground; YouTube was created; and after a seven-year legal battle, which became a fervent cause for pro-life activists, Terry Schiavo, who had been in a vegetative state, had her feeding tube removed and died.

They were sixteen in 2006 when Twitter, the morning-after pill, and the film *An Inconvenient Truth*, about global warming appeared; North Korea carried out its first nuclear weapons test; and the UN Security Council imposed sanctions on Iran for enrichment of nuclear materials.

They were seventeen in 2007 when Nancy Pelosi became the first female speaker of the US House of Representatives; a student killed thirty-two schoolmates and wounded twenty-five others at Virginia Tech; the iPhone was unveiled; and the Dow Jones Industrial Average hit a peak of 14,198.

They were eighteen in 2008 when they completed high school and began college; the United States and much of the rest of the world plunged into a deep recession; the major banking, insurance, and investment houses teetered at the edge of bankruptcy as a consequence of subprime mortgages; Lehman went over the edge; federal stimulus and bailout programs followed; Barack Obama—young, multiracial, charismatic, calling for change and bipartisanship—was overwhelmingly elected president; unemployment and housing foreclosures continued to climb as the stock market and the availability of credit declined; the Tea Party, a conservative and Libertarian grassroots organization seeking to reduce taxes, curb government spending, and scale back government, was forming; and terrorists held Mumbai, India, hostage for three days, killing 164 and wounding 308.

They were nineteen in 2009 when Sonia Sotomayor, the first Latina, was named to the US Supreme Court; Bernard Madoff was convicted of the largest Ponzi scheme in US history; and the Dow Jones Industrial Average reached a low of 6547.

They were twenty in 2010 when national health care was signed into law; a British Petroleum oil platform caught fire and sank, spewing more than 170 million gallons of oil in the Gulf of Mexico over a three-month period; Arizona adopted the most far-reaching immigration law in the United States, seeking to identify, prosecute, and deport illegal aliens; and a 7 magnitude earthquake caused catastrophic damage and death in Haiti.

They were twenty-one in 2011 when the Arab Spring brought revolutions in Egypt and Tunisia, a civil war in Libya, uprisings in Yemen and Syria, and protest across much of the Middle East, powered by Twitter and Facebook; Osama bin Laden was killed; an 8.9 magnitude earthquake caused massive damage, deaths, tsunami, and a nuclear accident in Japan; NATO intervened on behalf of rebels in the Libyan civil war; oil prices reached a high of nearly $150 a barrel; the Dow broke 12,000; and US troops withdrew from Iraq.

Studies Used in This Book

THE DATA used in this book, as well as its predecessors *When Hope and Fear Collide* (1998) and *When Dreams and Heroes Died* (1980), were drawn principally from three sources.

One source was undergraduate surveys conducted in 1969, 1976, 1993, and 2009. They examined college student attitudes, values, and experiences. The 1969 survey of a representative sample of twenty-five thousand undergraduates was conducted under the auspices of the Carnegie Commission on Higher Education with the cooperation of the American Council on Education with support from the US Office of Education. The 1976 survey, again a representative sample of twenty-five thousand undergraduates, was carried out by the Carnegie Council on Policy Studies in Higher Education. The 1993 survey of a representative sample of 9,100 undergraduates was conducted for Arthur Levine and Jeanette Cureton by the Opinion Research Corporation of Princeton, New Jersey. The 2009 survey of a representative sample of five thousand undergraduates was carried out by coauthor Diane Dean and her colleagues at the Illinois State University. Additional information on the survey—its methods, questionnaire, sampling, demographics, response rates (50 percent), and data treatments—are available from Diane Dean, Department of Educational Administration and Foundations, College of Education, Illinois State University,

Normal, Illinois 61790. In all four surveys, the data collected were weighted to reflect the composition of American higher education by institutional type, location, and control as well as student demographics, among other variables.

The second source of data was surveys of senior student affairs officers conducted in 1978, 1992, 1997, 2008, and 2011. They focused on the characteristics of the students attending their colleges and universities, campus policies and practices, events and activities, student attitudes and behaviors, and changes experienced over the years. In 1978, under the auspices of the Carnegie Council, surveys were sent to a representative sample of 586 senior student affairs officers. As with the undergraduate surveys, these questionnaires included short-answer and open-ended items. In 1992, Jeanette Cureton and Arthur Levine sent an updated version of the questionnaire to the senior student affairs officers at a representative sample of 270 institutions of higher education. A follow-up survey was administered to the same colleges and universities during the 1996–1997 academic year. The 2008 survey, also targeting 270 campuses, was administered by coauthor Diane Dean and her colleagues at the Illinois State University. Additional information regarding the survey—its methods, questionnaire, sampling, demographics, response rates (59 percent), and data treatments are available from Diane Dean. In summer 2011, the findings were updated by surveying the senior student affairs officers at the twenty-six institutions (twenty-five responded) where we had conducted site visits between 2007 and 2008.

Campus site visits were the third major source of data. They were conducted at a set of colleges and universities designed to represent the diversity of US higher education in terms of their size, control, location, degree level, demographics, and religious orientation. Each site visit included interviews with the senior student affairs officer and often staffers, the student government president, the student newspaper editor, and focus groups of students, ranging from a handful to a score of diverse students. There were also informal conversations with students and less frequently faculty members and campus walk-abouts, which were not in any way standardized but might include information gathered from bulletin boards, student centers, graffiti, libraries, bookstores, and dormitories. Beyond the interviews, documentation included reports, student newspapers, fliers, and just about anything else we could get our hands on. *When Dreams and Heroes Died* relied on twenty-six campus site visits; *When Hope and Fear Collide* entailed twenty-eight site visits. This book evaluated twenty-six campuses. In the course of the research, thirty-one colleges and universities were actually visited, but five were employed as test sites to assess the interview protocols and train the interviewers. A list of the thirty-one institutions can be found in Appendix C.

Of course, this study relied on many other sources and those are cited in the text. The research of the 1990s, which resulted in *When Hope and Fear Collide*, was supported by a grant from the Lilly Endowment. This book was funded by the Lumina Foundation.

Campus Contacts

THIRTY-ONE COLLEGES and universities assisted us in preparing for and carrying out campus site visits. These institutions assisted us in the development of the instruments employed in the site visits, tests and pilots of those instruments, and the actual site visits. On each campus there were one or more liaisons who made our work possible. They did everything from assembling groups of colleagues to reviewing our plans, testing our questionnaires, participating in trial interviews, and scheduling visits, which entailed interviews with senior student affairs officers, student government leaders, student newspaper editors, and student focus groups. We are very grateful to each and every one of those liaisons. This book rests heavily on the work they did.

Alabama State University; Montgomery, Alabama
Charles Smith, vice president for student affairs

Alamo Community College District; San Antonio, Texas
Lina Silva, vice chancellor for student services
Patricia Candia, vice president of student success, St. Phillips College
Debbie Hamilton, vice president for student success, Northeast Lakeview College

Cynthia Mendiola-Perez, director of student support services, Palo Alto College

Diane Muniz, vice president for student success, Northeast Vista College

Robert Vela, dean of student affairs, San Antonio College

Arizona State University; Phoenix, Arizona
Luoluo Hon, dean of student affairs, west campus
Patricia Arredondo, university dean of student affairs, Tempe campus
Dr. Kevin Cook, dean of student affairs, downtown campus
Gary McGrath, dean of student affairs, polytechnic campus

Berea College; Berea, Kentucky
Gail Wolford, vice president for labor and student life

College of Dupage; Glen Elyn, Illinois
Kay Nielsen; vice president for student affairs

Colorado State University; Fort Collins, Colorado
Blanche Hughes, vice president for student affairs

Illinois Wesleyan University; Bloomington, Illinois
Kathy Cavins-Tull, vice president for student affairs and dean of students

Kapi'olani Community College; Honolulu, Hawaii
Mona Lee, dean of students

Iowa State University; Ames, Iowa
Thomas Hill, vice president for student affairs

Lewis and Clark College; Portland, Oregon
W. Houston Dougharty, dean of students

Miami Dade Community College; Miami, Florida
Norma Martin Goonen, provost for academic and student affairs
Armando Ferrer, dean of students, Kendall campus
Malou Harrison, dean of students, north campus
Herbert Robinson, dean of students, Wolfson campus

Mt. Holyoke College; South Hadley, Massachusetts
Elizabeth Braun, dean of students

Mt. St. Mary's College; Los Angeles California
Jane Lingua, vice president for student affairs

Oberlin College; Oberlin, Ohio
Linda Gates, dean of students

Pepperdine University; Malibu, California
Mark Davis, dean of student affairs

Pikes Peak Community College; Colorado Springs, Colorado
Corlette Berge, interim vice president for student services

Princeton University, Princeton, New Jersey
Janet Smith Dickerson, vice president for campus life

Purdue University; West Lafayette, Indiana
Thomas B. Robinson, vice president for student affairs

Rollins College; Winter Park, Florida
Donna Lee, dean of students

St. Ambrose University; Davenport, Iowa
Tim Phillips, associate vice president and dean of students

San Diego Community College District; San Diego, California
Barbara Kavalier, dean of student affairs, Mesa College
Peter Fong, vice president for student services, Miramar College

Swarthmore College; Swarthmore, Pennsylvania
James Larimore, dean of students

Truman State University; Kirksville, Missouri
Lou Ann Gilchrist, dean of students

University of Alaska; Fairbanks, Alaska
Timothy Barnett, vice chancellor for student and enrollment services

University of California, Santa Barbara; Santa Barbara, California

Michael Young, vice chancellor for student affairs

University of Georgia; Athens, Georgia

Rodney Bennett, vice president for student affairs

University of Nevada; Las Vegas, Nevada

Rebecca Mills, vice president for student affairs

University of Texas, El Paso; El Paso, Texas

Richard Padilla, vice president for student affairs

University of Wisconsin, Milwaukee; Milwaukee, Wisconsin

Helen Marmarchev, vice chancellor for student affairs

Vanderbilt University; Nashville, Tennessee

Mark Bandas, associate provost and dean of students

Westchester Community College; Valhalla, New York

Joseph Hankin, president

REFERENCES

Adams, H. (2009). The education of Henry Adams. In *The collected works of Henry Adams*. Halcyon Classics Series [Kindle version]. Retrieved from http://www.amazon.com/ Collected-Unexpurgated-Halcyon-Classics-ebook/dp/ B00318DBKO#reader_B00318DBKO

Alch, M. L. (2000, September 1). The echo-boom generation: A growing force in American Society. *The Futurist, 34*(5), 42.

Boone, J. A. (2000). *Queer frontiers: Millennial geographies, genders, and generations*. Madison: University of Wisconsin Press.

Burke, E. (1967). Reflections on the revolution in France. In R. J. Hoffman (Ed.), *Burke's politics: Selected writings and speeches of Edmund Burke on reform, revolution and war* (p. 318). New York: Knopf. (Originally published in 1790.)

CIRCLE. (2008, December 19). *Young voters in the 2008 presidential election*. Medford, MA: Author.

CIRCLE. (2009, September). The youth vote 2008. *Around the CIRCLE, 6*(2). Medford, MA.

College Board. (2011). Average published tuition and fee charges in constant dollars 1981–82 to 2010–11. In *Trends in college prices*. New York: Author.

The Digital Future Project. (2011). *The digital future project 2011*. Los Angeles: Center for the Digital Future, University of Southern California, Annenberg School.

Dolby, N. (2012). *The new empathy: Developing multicultural and global consciousness in the millennial generation.* London: Routledge.

Elmore, T., & Cathy, D. (2010). *Generation iY: Our last chance to save the future.* Atlanta: Poet Gardner Publishing.

Emerson, R., & Perry, B. (1926). *The heart of Emerson's journals.* Boston: Houghton Mifflin.

Friedman, T. L. (2005). *The world is flat.* New York: Farrar, Straus, and Giroux.

Gallup International. (1969). *Gallup opinion index report 1969.* Princeton, NJ: Author.

Gibson, C., & Jung, K. (2002, September). *Historical census statistics on population totals by race, 1790 to 1990, and by Hispanic origin, 1970 to 1990, for the United States regions, divisions, and states.* Working Paper Series No. 6. Washington, DC: US Census Bureau.

Hartley, L. P. (1953). *The Go-Between.* New York: New York Review Books Classics.

Hopkins, M. (2005). *Save generations Y and Z.* Bloomington, IN: AuthorHouse.

Howe, N., & Strauss, W. (1992). *Millennials rising: The history of America's future, 1584–2069.* New York: Vintage Books.

Humes, K. R., Jones, N. A., & Ramirez, R. R. (2011, March). *Overview of race and Hispanic origin: 2010.* Washington, DC: US Bureau of the Census.

Immerwahr, J. A. (2010). *Squeeze play 2010: Public attitudes about college access and affordability.* New York: Public Agenda.

Institute of Politics. (2011). *Survey of young Americans' attitudes towards politics and public service.* Cambridge, MA: Harvard Institute of Politics.

Institute on International Education. (2010). *Open doors 2010.* New York: Author.

Irving, W. (2011). *Rip Van Winkle* [Kindle version].

Jukes, I. M. (2010). *Understanding the digital generation: Teaching and learning in the new digital landscape.* Seattle: Create Space.

Lancaster, L. C. (2010). *The m-factor: How the millennial generation is rocking the workplace.* New York: HarperBusiness.

Levine, A. (1980). *When dreams and heroes died: A portrait of today's college students.* San Francisco: Jossey-Bass.

Levine, A., & Cureton, J. (1998). *When hope and fear collide: A portrait of today's college students.* San Francisco: Jossey-Bass.

Levine, A., & Scheiber, L. (2010). *Unequal fortunes: Snapshots from the Bronx.* New York: Teachers College Press.

Lewin, T. (2011, November 2). College graduates' debt burden grew, yet again, in 2010. *New York Times.* Retrieved from. www.NYtimes.com/2011/11/03/education/average-student-loan-debt-grew-by-5-percent-in-2010-html_r1&emc=eta1

Lipkin, N. A. (2009). *Y in the workplace: Managing the "me first" generation.* Pompton Plains, NJ: Career Press.

Main Circle. (2010, February). *Vassar's activist groups.* Poughkeepsie, NY: Vassar College.

Mather, M., Pollard, K., & Jacobsen, L. A. (2011, July). *Reports on America.* Washington, DC: Population Reference Bureau.

McHaney, R., & Daniel, J. (2011). *The new digital shoreline: How web 2.0 and millennials are revolutionizing higher education.* Sterling, VA: Stylus Publishing.

Miller, C. K. (2003). *Making God Real for a new generation: Ministry with millennials born from 1982 to 1999.* Colorado Springs. Discipleship Resources.

Milner, H. (2010). *The Internet generation: Engaged citizens or political dropouts*. Medford, MA: Tufts University Press.

National Center for Education Statistics. (2010). Table 282: Bachelor's degrees conferred by degree-granting institutions, by field of study, selected years, 1970–71 through 2008–09. *Digest of Education Statistics*. Washington, DC: Author. Retrieved from www.nces.ed.gov/programs/digest/d10/tables/dt10_282.asp

National Center for Institute of Education Sciences. (2011). Table 3: Time to degree: Median and percentage distribution of 2007–08 first-time bachelor's degree recipients by number of months from enrollment to degree attainment and enrollment characteristics: 2009. *2008–09 baccalaureate and beyond longitudinal study (B&B:08/09)* (pp. 10–11). Washington, DC: Author. Retrieved from http://nces.ed.gov/pubs2011/2011236.pdf

Nelson, L. A. (2011, November 15). *Occupy student loans*. Inside Higher Education. Retrieved from http://www.insidehighered.com/news/2011/11/15/occupy-protests-focusing-increasingly-student-debt

Office of Immigration Statistics. (2011). Persons obtaining legal permanent resident status by region and selected country of last residence: Fiscal year 1820 to 2010. *2010 yearbook of immigration statistics*. Washington, DC: US Department of Homeland Security.

Palfrey, J., & Gasser, U. (2010). *Born digital: Understanding the first generation of digital natives*. New York: Basic Books.

Peterson, R., & Bilurosky, J. A. (1971). *May 1970: The campus aftermath of Cambodia and Kent State*. Berkeley, CA: Carnegie Council on Policy Studies in Higher Education.

Petit, P. (2008). *Man on a wire*. New York: Sky Horse Publishing.

Pew Internet and American Life Project. (2011). *Generations and their gadgets*. Washington, DC: Pew Research Center.

Pew Research Center. (2010). *Millennials: A portrait of generation next*. Washington, DC: Author.

Pew Social Trends Center. (2010, June 30). *How the great recession has changed life in America*. Retrieved from http://www.pewsocialtrends.org/2010/06/30/how-the-great-recession-has-changed-life-in-america/

President's Commission on Higher Education. (1947). *Higher education for American democracy: The president's commission on higher education*. New York: Harper & Row.

Pryor, J. H. (2007). *The American freshman: Forty year trends*. Los Angeles: Cooperative Institutional Research Program, University of California, Los Angeles.

Pryor, J. H., & DeAngelo, L. B. (2010). *The American college freshman: National norms fall 2010*. Los Angeles: Cooperative Institutional Research Program, University of California, Los Angeles.

Rowling, J. K. (1997). *Harry Potter and the sorcerer's stone*. New York: Scholastic.

Russell, B. (1961). *The basic writings of Bertrand Russell* [Google edition].

Tapscott, D. (2008). *Grown up digital: How the net generation is changing your world*. New York: McGraw-Hill.

Trilling, B., & Fadel, C. (2009). *21st century skills: Learning for life in our times*. San Francisco: Jossey-Bass.

Tulgan, B. (2009). *Not everyone gets a trophy: How to manage generation Y*. San Francisco: Jossey-Bass.

US Administration on Aging. (2008). *The older population by age group, sex, race and Hispanic origin*. Washington, DC: Author.

Retrieved from www.aoa.gov/aoaroot/aging_statistics/. . ./
popAGE1900–20150-by-decade.xls

US Bureau of Labor Statistics. (2011, April 8). *College enrollment
and work activity of 2010 high school graduates.* Washington,
DC: Author.

US Census Bureau. (2002, September 13). *United States—race and
Hispanic origin: 1790 to 1990.* Retrieved from www.census.
gov/population/www/documentation/twps0056/tab01.pdf

Vanderhaagen, D. A. (2005). *Parenting the millennial generation:
Guiding our children born between 1982 and 2000.* Westport,
CT: Praeger.

Watkins, S. C (2009). *The young and the digital: What the migra-
tion to social network sites, games, and anytime, anywhere media
means for our future.* Boston: Beacon Press

We are the 99 percent. (2011, November). OccupyWallSt.org.

Winograd, M., & Hais, M. D. (2009). *Millennial makeover:
Myspace, YouTube, and the future of American politics.* New
Brunswick, NJ: Rutgers University Press.

Zoba, W. M. (1999). *Generation 2K: What parents and others need
to know about millennials.* Downers Grove, IL: InterVarsity
Press.

INDEX